One of the most outstanding European Christians there has ever been' is David Bentley-Taylor's appreciation of Erasmus, and he is absolutely right. His seminal writings were indispensable to the sixteenth-century Reformers, and he deserves to be better known – and to be more widely enjoyed. Contemporaries called this razor-sharp writer one of the wonders of the world. This attractive presentation of him is painted largely in his own words from his masterly letters. David Bentley-Taylor himself has a pleasantly direct style which lays before us the many-sided genius of Erasmus in an easily accessible form. This is a sympathetic portrayal which will introduce many to the first Christian intellectual to command a truly European audience.

Professor David Wright
New College, Edinburgh

D1411471

My Dear Erasmus

The Forgotten Reformer

David Bentley - Taylor

Christian Focus

Copyright © David Bentley-Taylor 2002

ISBN 1 85792 695 1

Published in 2002 by
Christian Focus Publications,
Geanies House, Fearn, Ross-shire
IV20 1TW, Great Britain

www.christianfocus.com

Cover design by Alister MacInnes

Printed and bound by
Cox & Wyman, Reading, Berkshire

All rights reserved. No part of this publication may be reproduced, stored in a retrieval system, or transmitted, in any form, by any means, electronic, mechanical, photocopying, reocrding or otherwise without the prior permission of the publisher or a license permitting restricted copying. In the U.K. such licenses are issued by the Copyright Licensing Agency, 90 Tottenham Court Road, London W1P 9HE

Contents

The Greatness of Erasmus

Erasmus in childhood	an academic orphan
Erasmus in maturity	linguist and scholar
Erasmus in his prime	a chronic invalid
Erasmus in Europe	an international traveller
Erasmus at home	a tireless correspondent
Erasmus at work	author, editor, translator
Erasmus and the classics	an enthusiastic student
Erasmus and young people	an invaluable teacher
Erasmus and the New Testament	translator; expositor
Erasmus and Jesus Christ	a diligent disciple
Erasmus and morality	Christ's teaching
Erasmus and the Popes	critic; optimist
Erasmus and the Roman Catholic Church	rebel; reformer
Erasmus and the Reformation	the forerunner

Preface

Erasmus was thirty years old in 1500, so it might not seem surprising that he is little known today. Yet to many of his contemporaries he was the greatest man alive, the modern Socrates, whose learning and wisdom had not been equalled for a thousand years, 'a kind of divine being sent down to us from heaven'.

They may not have been altogether wrong, for in 1969 the University of Toronto Press began to publish the 'Collected Works of Erasmus' in English in 86 volumes. By the dawn of the new millennium half of them were already in print, including eleven which record his surviving correspondence up to 1525.

Those eleven volumes, four thousand pages of letters written by him or to him, are the prime source of this book. My aim has been to discover from them the convictions he held and advocated before he was eclipsed by Luther. For the march of history has not been kind to Erasmus. In spite of his phenomenal achievements he has been forgotten, concealed behind the Reformation.

He corresponded on a massive scale with the leaders of society all over western Europe apart from Scandinavia, with kings and popes, with cardinals, bishops and theologians, with professors and headmasters, with philosophers, humanists and doctors, with businessmen, administrators, bankers and lawyers, along with a host of intellectuals influenced by his writings, who became colleagues or critics of his daring research into the human condition and its responsibilities.

Quotations are identified by letter number and line number, while the Index of Selected Subjects enables his thinking on moral, spiritual and theological issues to be investigated.

I am indebted to my wife Felicity for much helpful advice and to Dr. R. M. Schoeffel of the University of Toronto Press for his encouragement.

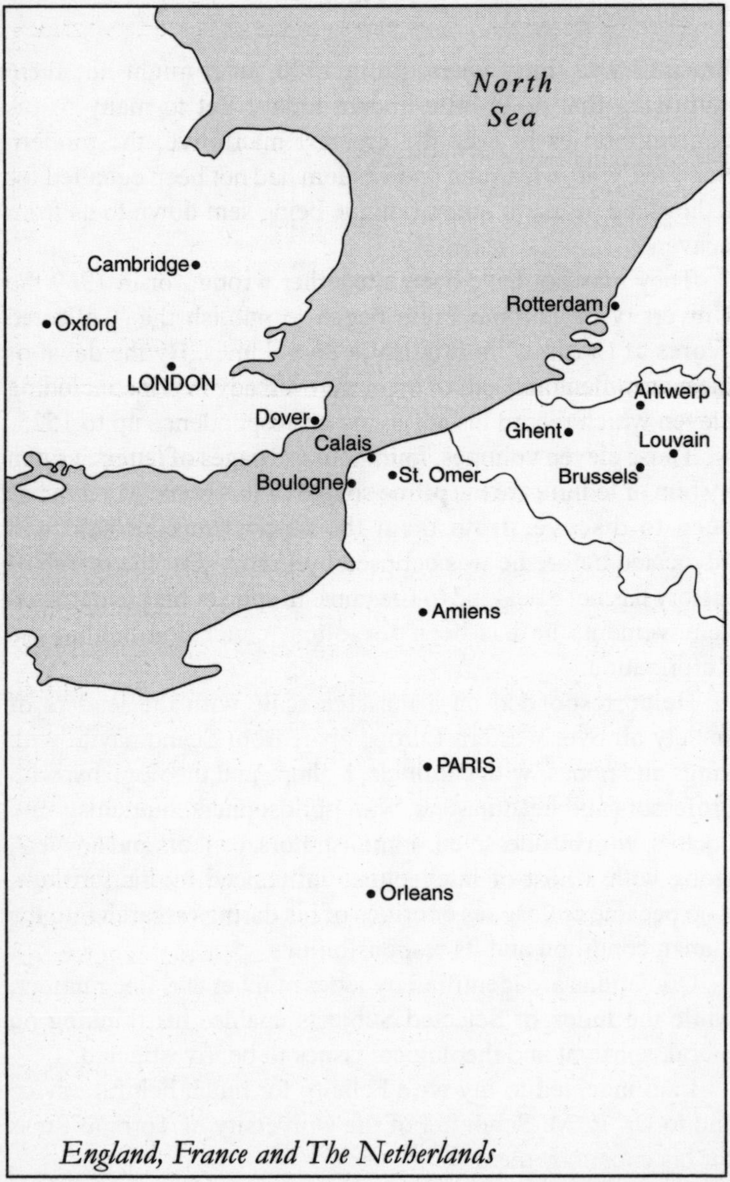

England, France and The Netherlands

1

The Emerging Scholar

Latin and printing;
Jerome; Mountjoy; Colet; *Adages*.

1469-1500: Netherlands, Paris, London, Oxford

Erasmus was born in 1469 at Rotterdam in the Netherlands. His parents had not been married, for his father was a Catholic priest. Both died when he was thirteen but, although denied secure home life, he was from childhood exceptionally intelligent. 'Swept away by some natural force, when I was playing with my toys I was already an academic' (447:261-2). At school he learnt Latin, which appealed to him so much that he made it his own language, virtually abandoning Dutch. 'When I was a boy the study of classical literature had begun among the Italians, but because the printer's art was known to very few, nothing in the way of books came through to us, and unbroken slumber graced the universal reign of those who taught ignorance in place of knowledge. The former teacher of my own teacher, well acquainted with Greek as well as Latin, was the first to bring us a breath of purer learning out of Italy. As a boy of twelve or so, I was blessed with a sight of him, but that was all, and yet a kind of secret natural force swept me into liberal studies. My teachers might forbid it; even so, I furtively drank in what I could from such books as I had managed to acquire. I practised my pen and I used to challenge my companions to compete with me. In boyhood my preference for verse was such that it was with reluctance I turned to prose: there was no form of poetry which I did not attempt' (1341A:31-45, 66-70 and 23:58-65).

His guardians proposed he should become a monk, but 'my mind was attracted solely to literature' (296:20) and he longed to go to a university. However, a monk related to him urged him to share his life, pointing out that there was a fine library in the monastery. Together they began to study the writings of Terence, the pre-Christian Roman comedian, and then for several months read other classical authors extensively in furtive nocturnal sessions. And so it came about that his guardians got their way and Erasmus, contrary to his real wishes, was absorbed into a monastic order. After a probationary year he had to conform to customs and ceremonies 'utterly repugnant to my mind and body alike, to my mind because I disliked ritual and loved freedom, to my body because I could not tolerate its hardships', such as fasting and broken nights (296:30-35). 'I will not deny that I had a tendency to grievous faults, but literary studies kept me from many vices. I have never been a slave to pleasures, though I was once inclined to them. Drunkenness and debauchery have always disgusted me and I have avoided them' (296:42-56).

He remained in the monastery for several years, reading very widely. Then he became secretary to a French bishop, so it was not until 1495, when he was 26 years old, that he entered the university of Paris. And by that time he had educated himself so thoroughly that he was more a teacher than a learner, inspiring others not only by his warm friendship and disciplined life but also by his encyclopaedic knowledge of Latin language and literature, including Church Fathers as well as classical authors. 'Jerome was a favourite in my adolescence,' he said later (1451:154), and 'when I was a boy Cicero attracted me less than Seneca. I was almost twenty before I could bear to read Cicero at any length, although I liked almost all other writers' (1390:113-115).

In his time, western Europe was dominated by the Catholic Church, whose bishops, priests, monks, and monasteries were prominent all over the continent. Inheriting this tradition, so powerful and successful for over a thousand years, Erasmus was automatically Christianized, but during the century in which he was born that great renewal of the mind known as the Renaissance had influenced the thinking of the intelligentsia. Impressive pre-Christian Latin and Greek writings had been rediscovered, encouraging scholars to go back to earlier sources and quickening a sense that medieval ecclesiastical authors did not have a monopoly of wisdom. A new humanism had developed which was not anti-Christian but laid its emphasis on man rather than God, on earth in preference to heaven, and on secular interests instead of predominantly religious considerations.

And the international language of Christendom was Latin. Boys who went to school spent a lot of their time not only in mastering Latin grammar and literature but also in learning to speak it. So educated people, no matter where they came from or what their mother tongue, could talk to one another and write to one another in Latin. Though he was studying in Paris, Erasmus needed only a smattering of French, for the University used Latin.

In addition to this linguistic unity, Erasmus had the good fortune to be born fifteen years after the invention of printing. By the time he was needing them a new race of technicians had arisen, the great early printers, putting an end to the countless centuries when every single book had to be written out separately by hand. So, as the year 1500 approached, the prevailing religious uniformity, the opening of minds thanks to the Renaissance, the Latin language, and the printers offered a wide prospect of influence which no one was to exploit more effectively than that unwanted boy who had been a scholar from the cradle.

About thirty of the letters he wrote as a teenager have survived the centuries. 'For some inexplicable reason I do not become wearied by continuous letter-writing but am rather filled with an ardent desire to go on with it. The more I write, the more I wish to write.' He was well aware that 'the two famous Fathers of the Church, Augustine and Jerome, managed never to lack each other's presence because they exchanged letters, each placing his mind and feelings at the other's disposal' (23:4-15).

Alluding to 'the paths I myself have followed from boyhood', he gave advice to fellow-students in Paris. 'Your first endeavour should be to choose the most learned teacher you can find, for it is impossible that one who is himself no scholar should make a scholar of anyone else. As soon as you find him, make every effort to see that he acquires the feelings of a father towards you. Your friendship with him is of such importance as an aid to learning that it will be of no avail to you to have a tutor at all unless, by the same token, you have a friend. Secondly, be regular in your work. Regularity produces by daily practice a greater result than you would suppose. But nothing is worse than excess, so you should from time to time abate the strenuousness of your studies by recreation. Indeed, a constant element of enjoyment must be mingled with study, so that we think of learning as a game rather than drudgery. Remember to devote part of your time to silent thought; in addition, the contest of minds wrestling together is specially stimulating to the sinews of human understanding. Don't be ashamed to ask questions or to be put right. Avoid working at night. Daybreak is an excellent time for study. After lunch take some recreation or go for a walk. Just before you go to sleep read something of exquisite quality. Let sleep overtake you while you are musing on it and try to recall it when you wake. Choose the best authors for your reading, avoiding like the plague those who are lax and indecent, specially at your present time of life, which is instinctively lewd and prone less to follow the good than the evil way' (56, 63:37-43).

In his many surviving letters from those days he rarely mentioned God apart from formal expressions like 'God forbid', preferring to speak impersonally of Heaven, Providence, or Nature, occasionally of fate, or 'some deity'. When he recovered from a severe fever he was grateful 'for the aid of St. Geneviève, the famous virgin whose bones daily radiate miracles', and looking back over 'all the troubles that have from boyhood beset me' he professed not to be sure whether they were 'due to God's command or the influence of my birth-star' (50:5-7, 31:6-8), but in other moods persistent ill-health made him long for 'a life wherein I may in sanctified leisure devote all my time to God and meditate on holy writ' (74:6-8). 'As I reflect on the eminence of our friend Erasmus,' wrote an Italian lecturer in 1498, 'not only in learning but in a life transparently free from every vice, I cannot refrain from rejoicing. What is better or finer, or indeed more divine, than to discover so great a man, resplendent in dazzling gifts of both literary skills and moral character in this age of ours which is so slothful and corrupt, so detestable?' (84:1-15).

Though he claimed to set high value on the Bible (48:4), in his correspondence in these years he hardly ever referred to it apart from a few sayings of proverbial type such as 'a dog returns to its vomit'. He made no mention of what it teaches us to believe or do, yet in the same letters he quoted classical authors hundreds of times. Lines from Cicero, Virgil, Horace, Terence, Ovid, Juvenal, Quintilian, Seneca and Pliny sprang automatically to his mind. He advised people to carry Cicero's books everywhere with them as their constant companion, yet he scarcely mentioned the name of Christ.

He knew perfectly well that other young men in 'the dangerous phase of adolescence' (147:44-45) were 'wallowing in bestial self-indulgence without regard for decency or virtue, attending to dance and song as if we were born for play and amusement, roaming the streets by night, succumbing to drinking bouts and enslaved to mistresses, the most demanding tyrants of all' (35:54-69). But from his childhood he had enjoyed hard work and daily he reaped its benefits. 'I cannot admire you when the only thing you lack is the will to work,' he said to one of his friends. 'It is your own help you need first of all. You need expect no god or man to help you if you fail yourself. You must check and restrain the immoderate desires of your time of life, if you cannot altogether repress them, which is scarcely possible for a human being. You know what I mean' (15:4-66, 16:38-41).

He was criticised for advocating the plays of Terence by those who felt they contained nothing but immoral love affairs between young people which could only corrupt the reader's mind, but he disagreed. 'I am convinced that the comedies of Terence, read in the proper way, not only have no tendency to subvert men's morals but even afford great assistance in reforming them, for they inculcate the lesson that love is a most unhappy business, like a disease, treacherous, full of madness' (31:60-81). He maintained that true 'lovers of books are not those who keep their books on shelves and never handle them, but those who day and night thumb them, batter them, wear them out, and fill up the margins with notes' (31:35-38). That was how he had long been treating the works of Jerome, the outstanding Christian author living in Bethlehem eleven hundred years previously. 'To shock us out of our lethargy and awaken drowsy readers to study the inner meaning of the Scriptures, there is no class of author which Jerome did not use. Like a bee that flies from flower to flower, he collected the best of everything to make the honey stored in his books. I not only read his letters but copied all of them out with my own hands' (396:214-220, 22:22-23). Indeed Jerome became his model, his surrogate father.

Chronically short of funds, he made money by helping rich students in their work, including a young Englishman, Lord Mountjoy, who was to be tutor to the son of King Henry VII. In May 1499 Mountjoy took him over to London, where he not only met the nine year old boy who was one day to be Henry VIII but also Thomas More, the future Chancellor, who remained his close friend throughout life. And he spent two months in Oxford. John Colet, whose father had twice been Lord Mayor of London, had moved to Oxford after studying in Italy. 'It was here that I first knew him, for some good fortune had brought me there at the same time. He was about thirty, a few months younger than I. He was giving public lectures on all the Epistles of St. Paul' (1211:310-314). Having heard glowing reports of Erasmus in Paris, Colet invited him 'to share in this grand undertaking by lecturing on old Moses or on that elegant stylist Isaiah'. But Erasmus declined. 'I have learned to live with myself and I am only too well aware of my inadequacy. I am not yet qualified to work with you. Your proposal is too great for my powers. But nothing could afford me greater pleasure than daily debates between us on the subject of holy writ' (108:84-128).

In the course of these debates Erasmus revealed a wealth of Christian conviction and understanding impossible to deduce from his correspondence prior to 1500. He brilliantly corrected Colet on the meaning of Christ's words 'let this cup pass from me', insisting that they express 'a natural human aversion to death', for he was truly man as well as truly God, who then by his death reconciled fallen mankind to his Father, and as our redeemer revealed his love and mercy, setting us an example of obedience. 'Our Lord's purpose was to be a pattern of gentleness, mildness and patience' (109:62-3, 104-5).

Though he repeatedly differed from Colet during those few weeks, they became friends for life and Colet's letters were an inspiration to him. 'My dear Erasmus, of books and knowledge there is no end. Nothing can be better, in view of this brief life of ours, than that we should live a holy and pure life, using our best endeavours every day to become perfected. In my opinion we shall achieve this only by the fervent love and imitation of Jesus. Let us therefore take the short road to the truth. I mean to do this as far as in me lies' (593:18-25).

'I never found a place I like so much' was Erasmus' verdict after eight months in England, but as he was leaving the country on January 27, 1500, customs officers confiscated almost all the money he had hoped to take back to France. 'I lost twenty pounds on Dover beach, all I had in the world, shipwrecked before I even got on board.'

After crossing the Channel, he reached Amiens on his way to Paris, 'so exhausted from travelling that I was alarmed I might fall ill'. Noticing a signboard 'Horses for Hire', he turned in and the hirer was called. 'We agreed on a price, but he asked me what sort of currency he was to be given. I showed him the coins I had and he kept the finest for himself. I hired two horses and rode off about evening accompanied by a youth whom he claimed was his son-in-law, who was to bring the animals back. The beast on which I sat had a huge open sore on its neck. The youth asked permission to ride pillion behind me, saying the horse was used to carrying two riders. I allowed it and we began to talk of many things. He entertained no very high opinion of his father-in-law. The next day, long before nightfall we reached the village of Saint Just. I recommended going ahead but the youth made excuses, saying the horses should not be taxed beyond their strength. We had almost finished our supper when the servant-woman called the youth aside, alleging that one of the horses was in trouble. Then, to my great surprise, the hirer himself came into the dining-room. I asked what had happened. He said his daughter, the youth's wife, had been so severely kicked by a horse that she was almost at death's door. I began to detect an odour of fiction about this story and noticed a shiftiness in the hirer and dullness in the youth' (119;11-64), so he carefully barricaded his door that night. Such travels were invaluable to him, taking him away from his books and into the lives of ordinary people, whose experiences and thinking he was to capture so successfully in years to come.

Although he was not at all well in Paris after the hardships he had endured travelling on sea and land in winter, he succeeded in completing a book he had begun long before. 'As I was suffering from a persistent fever I had to dictate the work instead of writing it myself. Nevertheless I do not altogether despair, for I trust in St. Geneviève, whose ready help I have more than once enjoyed, particularly since I have also enjoyed the services of a highly-skilled physician. If we have received the gift of life from the Supreme Creator of the universe, yet it is by a physician's care that it is preserved. He, as it were, gives us our lives again, so he deserves to be regarded as a sort of god on earth' (124:15-19, 126:12-15).

This book, *Adages*, was to make him famous. A kind of summary of pre-Christian wisdom, it was a collection of 819 quotations, proverbs, and anecdotes out of the Latin classics, each with his own explanation and comments. In subsequent editions over many years he kept enlarging the book till it embraced 3,600 sayings. In due time the Venetian ambassador in London was to express the reaction of eminent people all over western Europe. 'I continue my daily reading of your *Adages* with the greatest pleasure, dear Erasmus, chuckling as I find myself throwing over all the things that used to satisfy me. And though the *Adages* you have got together are quite delightful, a great help to both learning and liveliness, yet what you add to them is far better still. The scholarship, the variety, the force, the abundance of the language, the delightful gaiety which beguiles the reader with its wit and refreshes his weariness, all this is quite extraordinary. If your work were compared with the classical writers, at no point would a fair-minded reader not prefer your modern inspiration to their ancient majesty. You have given so much new brilliance to the Latin language that I think you have done more to make it new and splendid than it has done to make you famous' (591:40-55, 66-68). Erasmus lived to see the book republished at least twenty-six times.

2

The Greek Language and the Christian Handbook

Lucian's satires; Valla's insights; theology and grammar

1500-1505: Paris, Louvain

For the rest of 1500 he remained in France. 'Perhaps you wonder what I am up to. My friends are my occupation and in their company, which I enjoy enormously, I refresh my spirits. They never thrust themselves upon me uninvited, but when I call for them they are at once at my disposal. I closet myself with them in some secluded nook. They speak when I ask them to speak, otherwise they keep silence. Their conversation lasts as long as I want. They go into every situation with me and I know they will stay with me to the very end of life. From time to time I exchange them, taking up first one and then another. It is their friendship which has made me perfectly happy. But in case my metaphor escapes you, you must understand that in all I have said about my friends I was speaking of my books' (125:14-44). This might suggest he was a recluse, cut off from normal life, but nothing could be further from the truth. He read people as brilliantly as he read books. 'I am by nature extremely prone to form friendships of all kinds' (52:30).

In April, while the *Adages* was being printed, he took one of the most important decisions of his life. 'I have turned my entire attention to Greek' (124:72). Long afterwards he recalled, 'I had a taste of Greek as a boy and returned to it when I was thirty years old' (1341A:223). Unable at first to afford a teacher, he found the language intensely difficult. 'My readings in Greek all but crush my spirit' (123:25, 139:128), but he had become convinced that 'a Latin education is imperfect without it' (129:78). Though he needed clothes, he gave priority to buying Greek books, for 'my mind is burning with indescribable eagerness to bring all my small literary works to their conclusion and to acquire a certain limited competence in the use of Greek and thereby go on to devote myself entirely to sacred literature' (138:50-54). This revealing statement was written at dawn on December 11 in Orléans, to which he had withdrawn when Paris was being ravaged by plague. And the Greek Erasmus pursued was not merely New Testament Greek but the whole language, classical, biblical, and spoken. In this he was deliberately following Jerome.

Back in Paris before Christmas he took up another demanding project. For more than ten years he had been enthusiastically studying Jerome's works, regarding him as the supreme champion of the faith, outstripping all other Christian writers and even rivalling Cicero. 'I have long had a burning desire to write a commentary on his letters and some god is now firing my spirit, impelling me to contemplate this massive enterprise, never before attempted by anyone. This is what I trust I may be able to do, provided the saint himself comes to my aid.' He hoped to make people so familiar with Jerome that they would read him and learn his works by heart in schools and churches and homes (141:18-20).

'One might ask why I want Greek at this age. I should be the happiest of men if in my boyhood I had formed such an intention. But, as I see it now, it is better to learn, even somewhat late, the things we ought to grasp first, than never to learn them at all. I can see what utter madness it is even to put a finger on that part of theology which is specially concerned with the mysteries of the faith unless one is furnished with Greek. Besides this, I am trying to restore the works of Jerome which have partly been corrupted, cut down, mutilated or filled with monstrous mistakes through ignorance of classical antiquity and of Greek; great Jerome, the only scholar in the church universal who had a perfect command of all learning both sacred and heathen. In this I recognise knowledge of Greek to be of first importance, so I have decided to spend several months with a Greek tutor' (149:11-27, 65-79).

In 1502 he could say 'the study of Greek absorbs me completely' (172:12) and in 1503 he produced a translation into Latin of some writings of Greek philosophers. 'These were my first ventures in this kind of work: I followed Cicero's old rule, to weigh the meaning, not count the words' (177:111-115). Soon he had made such phenomenal progress that 'I took in hand the translation of two tragedies by Euripedes, *Hecuba* and *Iphigenia in Aulis*. How much sweat this cost me only those who have stepped into the same wrestling-ring can understand. The very task of turning good Greek into good Latin demands exceptional skill, especially an author remarkably exquisite in style, in whom there is not a spare word or anything one could alter without doing him violence. I attempted to reproduce the shape and contours of the Greek poems, trying zealously to adapt the force of the meaning to Latin ears with all fidelity' (188:15-35, 60-63).

He then proceeded to consolidate this amazing self-imposed training by translating into Latin twenty-eight dialogues by the second century Greek satirist Lucian, grasping ever more clearly the immensely important task to which all this labour was the prelude. As though that were not enough, 'I began to take up Hebrew as well, but stopped because I was put off by the strangeness of the language, and at the same time the shortness of life. The limitations of human nature will not allow a man to master too many things at once' (181:41-45).

Lucian was important to him for another reason quite apart from his Greek. 'He satirizes everything with inexpressible skill and grace, ridicules everything and submits everything to the chastisement of his superb wit. He possesses such felicity of invention and such a charming sense of humour. By his mixture of fun and accurate observation he effectively portrays the manners, emotions and pursuits of men as with a painter's vivid brush yet also with a wisdom exceeding that which divines and philosophers commonly attain when they dispute over trifles, as certain persons do even today, cheating the population by conjuring up miracles, or with a pretence of holiness, or by feigned indulgences and other tricks of the kind' (193:33-34, 48-52, 64-66 and 199:9-12).

It was no wonder Lucian appealed to Erasmus. They were kindred spirits. In describing his genius, he was describing his own.

When plague again drove him from Paris, he spent a

year or more in the neighbourhood of Saint Omer. 'I have hidden myself away in the country, intending to brood in silence over holy writ during the winter months to come' (165:2-4). Winter travel gave him other experiences too, 'raging winds, biting cold, snow, trees bent over heavily laden with ice, the ground covered with ice as I sat, a terrified rider, on a terrified horse'. Then he found a better way. 'Since the wind blew hard from behind us, I slid down the slopes of the hills, sailing on the surface of the ice, from time to time steering with my staff, using it as a rudder. So wild was the weather, we scarcely met a soul, which brought us one advantage, we stood in less fear of attack by robbers, yet fear it we did' (88:25-42).

Though sometimes 'exhausted from the endless drudgery of writing' (176:3), he stuck determinedly to his task, 'writing books that may last forever' (139:43-44). Although 'dedicated to acquiring the most perfect scholarship I can, I am not unaware that the kind of study I pursue appears to some men as uncongenial, interminable, or unprofitable, yet this merely increases my ardour for it. I believe God will both approve it and aid it. And some day mankind, or at any rate posterity, will give me its approval' (161:32-45). Plague persisted and he was not surprised, for 'we daily provoke the Lord our God by greed, the parent of every crime, and by vices which have already well-nigh ceased to appear as vices, so common are they' (143:243-249). He moved into the southern Netherlands, today's Belgium, settling at the university town of Louvain, near Brussels. 'Hardly had I reached it when the magistrates invited me to give public lectures at the recommendation of Adrian of Utrecht, dean of Louvain', who twenty years later was to become Pope. 'I turned it down' (171:13-16).

It was while he was at Louvain that he published in February 1503 his first directly Christian work, *The Handbook of the Christian Soldier*, which was eventually to circulate in many editions and translations. 'I wrote it solely to counteract the error of those who make religion consist in rituals and observances but are astonishingly indifferent to matters that have to do with true goodness. What I have tried to do is to teach a method of morals' (181:53-58). It began with a summons to the reader to make war on vice and a warning that those who fail to do so will be plunged into hell. He asserted that the world around us, the enemy within us, and the devil himself keep us under incessant attack, luring our minds into deadly pleasures which lead to perdition and eternal night. But he was equally emphatic that God sent Christ to ransom us at the price of his blood, that the human body can become the temple of the Holy Spirit, and that our foes have already been conquered thanks to the death of Christ. 'Victory does not depend at all on chance but is entirely in the hands of God and through him also in our hands. No one fails to win in this battle except those who do not want to win, for a very important part of Christianity is to want to be a Christian with all your heart and soul. He will fight for you, but the victory will not come about without your effort' (CWE. Vol. 66. pp.29-30, 46:2).

In view of 'vestiges of the original sin of our first parents which remain in us even after baptism, obscuring and corrupting what had been so well put together by our Creator', Erasmus advocated the fervent study of Scripture. 'Of all the things you see with your eyes and touch with your hands, nothing is so true as what you read there. Meditation on a single verse will have more nourishment for you than the whole Psalter chanted monotonously. Christ answered the tempter with the words of divine Scripture' (pp.34:3, 35:2, 37:2). So Erasmus did the same, enforcing his message with texts such as 'There is no peace for the wicked' (Is. 57:21), 'The wages of sin is death' (Rom. 6:23), 'Put on the whole armour of God that you may be able to stand against the wiles of the devil' (Eph. 6:11), and 'We are more than conquerors through him who loved us' (Rom. 8:37). These he described as 'oracles which have issued from the holy of holies of the divine mind' (p.34:3). At the same time, 'I should certainly not disapprove a kind of preliminary training in the writings of the pagan poets and philosophers, provided one engages in these studies in moderation and only in passing. Cull what is best from the ancient authors and, like the bee flitting about the garden, suck out only the wholesome juice, leaving aside the poison. I advise you not to read the obscene poets at all' (pp.33:2, 36:2, 33:4).

He knew he was writing to people tormented by monstrous vices, blinded by the tyranny of their own emotions, and 'swayed by the fact that the majority of mankind live as if heaven and hell were some kind of old wives' fable' (p.55:2). Convinced that there is an art in living virtuously and eager to help his readers 'disentangle themselves from the errors of this world as from an inextricable labyrinth' (p.54:2), Erasmus passed from this long introduction to the main part of his *Handbook*, a system of twenty-two rules for living a truly Christian life, further reinforced by suggested remedies for six common temptations. Such a mass of exhortations does not make easy reading, though he intended it as 'a short way to Christ' (p.127).

He made it clear that he saw no value in pilgrimages to Rome, in lighting candles and prostrating yourself before statues, in having a tiny particle of the cross in your home, worshipping the bones of St. Paul in a casket of relics, gazing with awe at what was supposed to be the tunic of Christ, wearing religious clothes, observing a special diet, or trying to win God's favour by other observances as though they were magic rites. He deplored the extent to which professing Christians had become 'stuck in small things' (p.79:3), ascribing great importance to what was worthless while disregarding what was really important – the fruit of the Holy Spirit in their daily lives. 'Being sprinkled with a few drops of holy water is useless unless you clean up the inner defilement of the soul' (p.71:2). Immersed in study as he was, he was well aware of what was going on in the allegedly Christian society all around him. 'When was debauchery more unchecked? When was fornication and adultery more widespread, more unpunished, or less a source of disgrace?' (pp.86-87). And he felt that confessing vicious habits time and again to a priest was not to be compared with hating and abandoning them for good. 'The young should be advised not to defile their lives with vice before they know what life is. When a mad youth is dying for love of a girl, the common crowd calls that love, yet there is no hatred more cruel than this. He does not love the girl but himself, although he does not really love even himself' (p.105).

He was concerned that priests who celebrated mass daily still lived selfish lives and had never sacrificed themselves to Christ, while people buoyed up by the ceremony failed to reflect on what it really represented. 'God will hate your flabby religion. In private you are more pagan than pagans' (pp.70-71). He wanted evidence that they had been inwardly buried with Christ and were living a new life before he could recognise them as Christians. He was at pains to explain that he did not entirely disapprove of ceremonies, recognising that they were almost a necessity for immature, simple-minded people. But he found most Christians 'superstitious rather than pious' (p.65:3), including the majority of priests and theologians, who 'observed silly little ceremonies, petty traditions invented by mere men', not only acquiring none of the 'qualities of Christ' but even lacking the common virtues that pagans often acquired through natural reason or the experiences of life or the precepts of philosophers (p.74). And he quoted from the first chapter of Isaiah to prove that God has no use for worship divorced from morality.

He admitted there were 'many monks who had some experience of the mysteries of the Spirit' (pp.77-78) but denounced 'that superstitious fraternity who try to thrust others into a monastic community as if Christianity did not exist outside the monk's cowl. Being a monk is not a state of holiness but a way of life, which may be beneficial or not according to each person's physical and mental constitution. I personally do not urge you to adopt it, nor yet do I urge you against it. I merely advise you to identify piety not with diet or dress or any visible thing but with what I have taught here' (p.127).

Then in the summer of 1504, 'as I was hunting in an ancient library, luck brought into my toils a prey of no ordinary importance, notes on the New Testament by Lorenzo Valla', the great Italian scholar of the previous century (182:4-6). Valla had translated some of the Greek classics into Latin, but his daring views on ethical and historical issues had made him unpopular. He had opposed the celibacy of the clergy – 'virginity is a mistake' – and the secular power of the Pope. Erasmus, who had profited from Valla's writings on Latin grammar, was now delighted to find him 'letting his pen loose on Holy Scripture itself', revealing deficiencies in the Latin Vulgate by comparing it with good Greek manuscripts. Some people thought it sinful to change anything in the Scriptures, but Erasmus knew that the text had often been corrupted by being copied out repeatedly through the centuries, so that such careful revision by a linguistically sensitive scholar was invaluable. 'This whole business of translating the Holy Scriptures is manifestly a grammarian's function. I do not really believe that Theology herself, the queen of all the sciences, will be offended if some share is claimed in her by her humble attendant Grammar; for, though Grammar is of less consequence in some men's eyes, no help is more indispensable than hers. She is concerned with small details, but details such as have always been indispensable for the attainment of greatness' (182:145-152).

And so in April 1505 he published in Paris his new edition of Valla's *Notes on the New Testament* which were to have such a significant influence on his own career. 'I am now eager to approach sacred literature full sail, full gallop', he told John Colet. 'I have an extreme distaste for anything that distracts me from it, or even delays me. Hereafter I intend to address myself to the Scriptures and to spend all the rest of my life upon them. So I beseech you to help me as far as you can in my burning zeal for sacred studies' (181:29-35, 85-86).

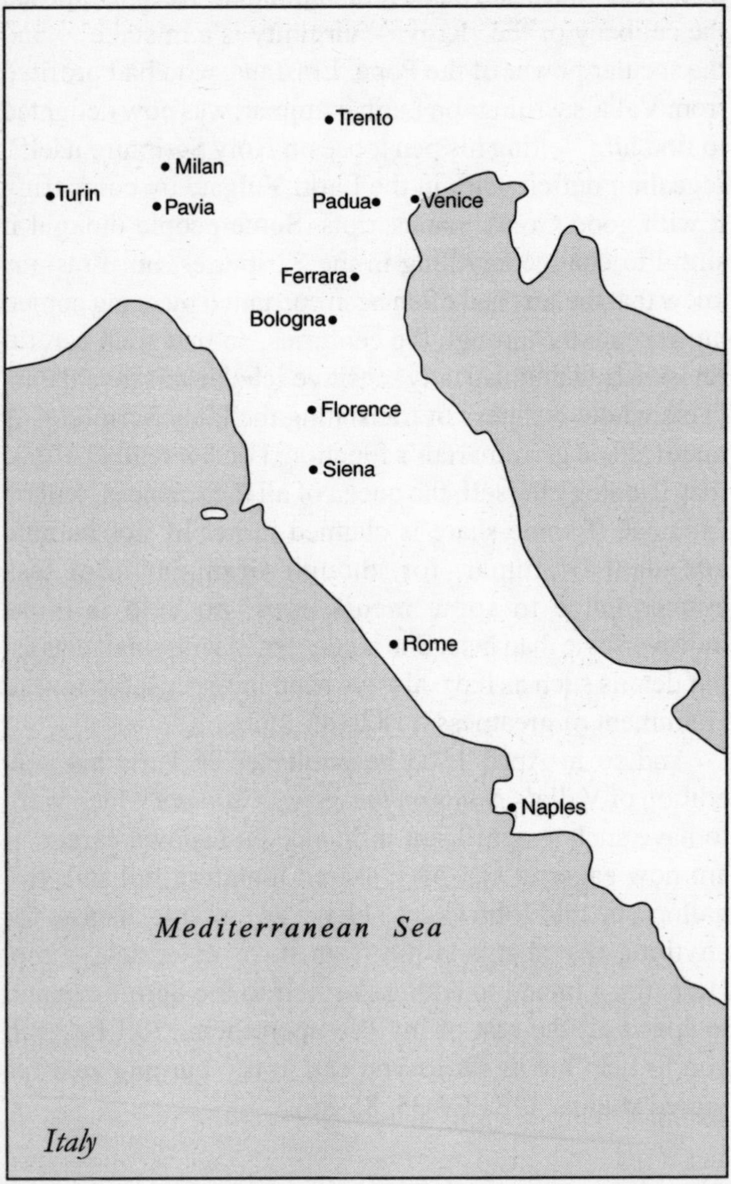
Trento
Milan
Turin
Pavia
Padua
Venice
Ferrara
Bologna
Florence
Siena
Rome
Naples
Mediterranean Sea
Italy

3

Misery, Kindness and Greek in Italy

Pope Julius' conquests; Venetian printer; leaving Rome

1506-1509: Bologna, Venice, Rome

In the autumn of 1505 he found himself writing letters from the bishop's palace in London. 'For the last few months I have been staying with my friend Lord Mountjoy, who pressingly invited me to come back to England' (185:12-24). For almost a year he was 'in high favour with the greatest men and finest scholars in the country' (189:4), including William Warham, the Archbishop of Canterbury, who became very attached to him. He collaborated with Thomas More in translating dialogues of Lucian from Greek into Latin, including one on friendship 'which has fallen into such deep neglect among Christians nowadays'. He reflected that 'Christianity itself is only that true and perfect kind of friendship which consists in dying with Christ, living in Christ, and forming one body and soul with Christ, a communion between men like that of limbs in the body' (187:24-29). He pondered on 'how I can wholly devote to religion and to Christ whatever life remains to me, for I am conscious how fleeting is life and how frail my own health' (189:7-10). Then suddenly, in June 1506, a wealthy Italian, King Henry VII's doctor, asked him to accompany his two sons to Italy, 'to keep an eye on them and steer them in their studies' (1341A:104). Erasmus was delighted, for he had been on the point of going to Rome seven years before, when Mountjoy first took him to England. So at short notice he returned to Paris. 'The sea voyage was horrible; for four nights we were at the mercy of wind and wave' (196:10-11). Travelling through France, they crossed the Alps to Turin. To relieve the tedium of the journey he composed a poem, 'scribbling it down from time to time on a piece of paper on my saddle-bow' and copying it out when they reached a 'dirty and uncomfortable inn' (1341A:97-98, 113-118 and 1352:22).

He spent the next three years in Italy, visiting Milan, Pavia, Florence, Padua, Ferrara and Naples rather briefly, 'staying several months in Siena for the benefit of my health', being in Bologna for a year, Venice for almost as long, then Rome for five months. 'I have come to Italy for many reasons,' he said, ten weeks after arriving, 'though I found her disturbed by the great tumult of the wars, so much so that, since the pope with the help of the French army was preparing to besiege Bologna, I was forced to leave and take refuge in Florence, turning dialogues of Lucian into Latin while I was escaping, rather than do nothing' (200:2-5, 205:39-40). But then he wrote from Bologna, 'I came to Italy mainly to learn Greek, but studies are dormant here at present, whereas war is hotly pursued, so I shall look for ways of hastening my return. I have taken a degree in theology. On November 11 Julius, the supreme pontiff, entered the city; the following Sunday he celebrated mass in the cathedral. Preparations are afoot for a war against the Venetians. Meanwhile all studies are in abeyance. Pope Julius is waging war, conquering, leading triumphal processions, in fact playing Julius to the life', by which Erasmus meant that the Pope was deliberately imitating Julius Caesar (203:3-15, 205:42-43).

We have only twelve of Erasmus' letters for this whole period of his life, seven of them extremely short and the other five concerned exclusively with his translations of Lucian and Euripedes or with a greatly enlarged edition of the *Adages*. There is not a single surviving letter from Rome, no account of his travels, nor of what he was doing or thinking, and not the slightest allusion to the Church in Italy, even when he was writing to the Archbishop of Canterbury. Yet Mountjoy referred to getting two letters from him, 'which brought me both pleasure and pain, because you confessed all your plans, thoughts, misfortunes and worries, your chapter of misery' (215:31-40), so it is evident that Erasmus felt it unwise to preserve most of the letters he wrote in those days.

Once his contract to the two boys was over, he was free to do as he liked. Although he had planned to move to Rome immediately after Christmas 1507, he changed his mind and went first to Venice, attracted not by its historic buildings and gondolas but by the fame of the Aldine Press established there by the remarkable Italian scholar-printer known as Aldus, who had made Greek the language of his household and issued in rapid succession not only large numbers of Latin works but one Greek classic after another. Erasmus was eager to have his translations of Euripedes into Latin reprinted by Aldus, attracted, as he told him, 'not only by your skill and by your type, which is unmatched for elegance, but also by your intellectual gifts and uncommon scholarship' (207:1-20). The attraction was mutual, for when Erasmus reached Venice in early January 1508 Aldus took him into his own home for the rest of the year, reprinted his Euripedes and then produced a new and bigger edition of the *Adages* in which the number of proverbs was increased to 3260, many of them from the Greek classics. It was this Aldine edition of 'my commentary on proverbs, a profane work of course but most helpful for the whole business of education' (269:111, 296:156), which made Erasmus known throughout Europe and prepared the way for the greater books he was yet to write.

To promote the study of Greek literature Aldus had launched the New Academy, whose members were committed to speaking Greek as well as sharing in the huge task of editing and publishing. Afterwards Erasmus recalled with pleasure some of the distinguished scholars 'whom I had the good fortune to see for myself', including the Cretan who gave lectures in Greek at 7 a.m. all the year round, on whose beautiful handwriting Aldus based the Greek text he used. 'One day when I was to have supper with the Cretan his little old father, who knew not a word of anything except Greek, was there. When it came to washing our hands, each of us made way for the other. So, to put an end to this pointless waste of time, I seized his father's hand and said in Greek, "We're the two old men", although I was not much older than his son. He was delighted and we washed our hands together' (1347:256-267). This happy experience of hard work and warm friendship in Venice crowned his prolonged study of the Greek language. Henceforth he could speak and use it as freely as he did Latin.

In early 1509 he at last reached Rome, where 'there was not a cardinal who did not welcome me as a brother', which is almost all we know about his time there. It can safely be presumed that he never met Pope Julius II, of whose military campaigns he disapproved so strongly that 'even to think of those days makes one's blood run cold' (335:142-3). Then on April 22 King Henry VII died in England and was succeeded by his son Henry VIII, aged 18, a budding scholar, linguist, musician and athlete. A month later Mountjoy wrote enthusiastically, "I am quite sure, my dear Erasmus, that, the moment you heard, every particle of gloom left your heart, for you are bound to repose the highest hopes in a prince whose exceptional and almost more than human talents you know so well. If you could see how excited everyone is here, how courageously and wisely he is acting, what a passion he has for justice and honesty and how warmly he is attached to men of letters, you would fly to us. Heaven smiles, earth rejoices, all is milk and honey. You are not merely our sovereign's acquaintance but his friend, for he has written to you in his own hand, as he has not done to many others. And the Archbishop of Canterbury promises you a benefice if you should return to England. He has just given me five pounds to send you for your travelling expenses, to which I have added another five. Enclosed with this letter you will find a bill of exchange for the money, so come back to us as soon as you can' (215:1-17, 75-93).

With such prospects set before him and his return fare so handsomely covered, Erasmus decided to go. Six years later he admitted to Cardinal Grimani that a very encouraging two hour conversation with him at his palace had almost induced him to remain in Rome. 'After that first meeting, which proved to be our last, I never revisited your Eminence, as you had told me to do and I had promised, and the reason for this was your special courtesy and kindness. The very thing that ought most to have encouraged me to return to you was the one thing that deterred me from doing so. I will explain frankly, as a good German should. At that time my mind was entirely made up to go back to England. It was to England that the ties of old acquaintance, the generous promises of influential friends, and the favourable attitude of a most successful King all summoned me. I had adopted the island to replace my native land. I had chosen it as the retreat for my old age. I was repeatedly invited in letters which promised me mountains of gold. And now I was afraid that if I paid a return visit to your Eminence I might change my mind. From the moment of our first meeting you had so weakened my resolution and so kindled my imagination, that I had begun to have some misgivings about my plans and yet I was ashamed to show myself a man of no strength of mind. I felt that my affection for the eternal city, which I had barely shaken off, was silently increasing once again, and that if I had not torn myself quickly away from Rome I should never have left it thereafter. I hurried away that I might not catch the infection a second time. And now you will ask, am I sorry that I did not take your advice? My feelings on this are by no means simple. A deep regret for Rome is inescapable, when I think of its great store of advantages. First of all, the bright light, the noble setting of the most famous city in the world, the delightful freedom, the many richly furnished libraries, the sweet society of all those great scholars, the many literary conversations, all the monuments of antiquity, and not least so many leading lights of the world gathered together in one place. All this makes me feel that no fortune could possibly fall to my lot generous enough to wean my heart from its longing for the Rome which I once tasted' (334:1-48).

Every word was true, but it was by no means the whole truth, as the best known of all his books was soon to reveal.

4

The Praise of Folly

Folly speaks; the ecclesiastical rebel

1509: London

It was a long ride from Rome to London but, since 1509 is the one year in Erasmus' adult life from which not a single letter has been preserved, we lack details about it, except that 'to avoid squandering in vulgar talk the whole time I had to spend on horseback I thought I must at all costs occupy myself somehow', so he started composing the book that was taking shape in his head. Several years passed before he explained what happened next. 'I was staying with More on returning from Italy, detained indoors for several days by pain in the kidneys. My books had not yet arrived, so to take my mind off my physical discomfort I began to amuse my idle moments with *The Praise of Folly*. I showed a specimen to several friends. They were highly delighted and urged me to continue. I spent a week on it, more or less. Then they carried it off to France, where it was printed, but from an imperfect copy. In a few months over seven editions were printed' (337:134-148). Its first words are 'Folly speaks'.

'What man would be willing to offer his neck to the halter of matrimony,' asks Folly, 'if he applied the usual practice of the wise man and first weighed up its disadvantages as a way of life? Or what woman would ever agree to take a husband if she thought about the pains and dangers of childbirth and the trouble of bringing up children? So, if you owe your existence to wedlock, you can see how much you owe to me, to Folly. From that game of mine, absurd as it is, spring haughty philosophers, monks, kings, priests, and thrice-holy pontiffs' (CWE. Vol. 27. p.90).

Setting off in this way, Folly ranges widely over human experience, proving it is she who makes life worth living. 'All the emotions belong to folly' (p.104). 'Nature confined reason to a cramped corner of the head and left all the rest of the body to the passions, swayed by folly' (p.95). 'A woman is always a woman, that is, a fool, whatever mask she wears. It's women's folly which makes them delight men' (p.95 and 96). 'What is there about babies which makes us hug and kiss and fondle them? Surely it is the charm of folly' (p.91). Having explained that 'the happiest group of people are those popularly called idiots, who are untroubled by the thousand cares to which our life is subject' (p.109), Folly surveys how much is owed to her by hunters, builders, gamblers, merchants, schoolmasters, poets, authors, lawyers, scientists, and in fact everyone. All this takes up more than half the book, with only an occasional glance at Christianity. Then Folly mentions 'those who enjoy deluding themselves with imaginary pardons for their sins, who rely on magic signs and prayers thought up by some pious impostor, promising themselves good health, long life, and finally a seat next to Christ in heaven' (p.114). She knows of 'many who set up a candle to the Virgin, but few emulate her chastity and love of heavenly things, which is surely the true way to worship, while others attribute more to the Mother of God than to her Son' (pp.120 and 115). 'Could anything be so foolish as those who promise themselves supreme bliss for repeating daily seven short verses of the Psalms? Things like this are so foolish that I almost blush for them myself, yet they win general approval. The ordinary life of Christians everywhere abounds in these varieties of silliness, encouraged by priests' (pp.115 and 114). Increasingly it becomes apparent that Folly is not really the only speaker. Erasmus admitted, 'I myself acted my part in disguise' (337:166). But then he virtually discarded disguise and boldly revealed his true feelings about the leadership of the Catholic Church at the close of his three years in Italy.

He surveyed 'our new breed of theologians', so dismayed by the nonsense they taught, 'polluting the majesty of divine theology by squalid trivialities', that he could not find a good word to say of them. Busy with their 'tomfooleries', they had no time to read the Gospels or Paul's letters, but 'refashioned the Holy Scriptures as though they were made of wax', discussing such absurdities as 'how, in the Eucharist, accidents can subsist without a domicile' or the exact moment when transubstantiation takes place, whereas the apostles never heard so much as a word on these matters from their Teacher. 'The apostles knew the mother of Jesus personally, but which of them proved how she had been kept immaculate from Adam's sin with the logic our theologians display? It had apparently never been revealed to them that a mediocre drawing sketched in charcoal on a wall should be worshipped in the same manner as Christ himself, provided that it had two fingers outstretched and three rays sticking out from the halo fastened to the back of its head' (pp.126-130).

He was equally merciless when it came to monks, 'most of them a long way removed from religion', often uneducated and ignorant, 'braying like donkeys in church, repeating the Psalms they haven't understood', frequently making a good living out of their squalor and begging. He ridiculed the rules they observed about the colour of their habit, the cut of their hair, the width of their girdles, and the shape of their cowls, trivialities which made them feel superior to others, and how they gloried in the names of their orders, 'as if it were not enough to be called Christians'. He deplored their emphasis on 'ceremonies and petty man-made traditions, yet they never think of the time to come when Christ will scorn all this and enforce his own rule of love' (pp.130-131).

'What shall I say about courtiers?' Folly went on. 'They sleep till midday, when a wretched little hired priest waiting at their bedside runs quickly through the mass. After that follows dice, draughts, fortune-telling, clowns, whores, idle games, dirty jokes. And such practices have long been zealously adopted, indeed almost surpassed, by supreme pontiffs, cardinals and bishops. If any of these were to reflect on the meaning of his linen vestment, snow-white to indicate a spotless life; or of his two-horned mitre, signifying perfect knowledge of both Old and New Testaments; of his hands protected by gloves, symbolic of purity for administering the sacrament; or the cross carried before him as a symbol of victory over all human passions – would he not lead a life as arduous as that of the original apostles?'

And then Folly dares to come to the most critical point of all. 'If the supreme pontiffs, the vicars of Christ, made an attempt to imitate his life of poverty and toil, his teaching, cross, and contempt for life, what creatures on earth would be so cast down? Who would want to spend all his resources on the purchase of their position, which once bought has to be protected by the sword, by poison, by violence of every kind? Think of all the advantages they would lose if they ever showed a sign of wisdom! Wisdom, did I say? Rather a grain of the salt Christ spoke of would suffice to rid them of all their wealth and honours, their sovereignty and triumphs, their many dispensations, taxes, and indulgences, all their horses and mules, their retinue, and their countless pleasures. (You'll note what a vast sea of profiteering I've covered in a few words.) In place of all this it would bring vigils, fasts, tears, prayers, sermons, study, sighs, and a thousand unpleasant hardships of that kind. Nor must we overlook what this will lead to. Countless scribes, copyists, clerks, lawyers, advocates, secretaries, muleteers, grooms, bankers and pimps (and I nearly added something rather more suggestive), in short, an enormous crowd of people now a burden on the Roman see would be left to starve. But as things are today, any work that has to be done they can leave to others, while claiming all the pomp and pleasure for themselves. Consequently, thanks to me, Folly, practically no class of man lives so comfortably with fewer cares, for they believe they do quite enough for Christ if they play their part by means of ritual, near-theatrical ceremonial and display, benedictions and anathemas, repeated excommunications and that dreaded thunderbolt whereby they can dispatch the souls of mortal men to the depths of hell. Teaching the people is too like hard work. Interpreting the Holy Scriptures is for scholastics. Praying is a waste of time. To be needy is hardly fitting for one who scarcely permits the greatest of kings to kiss his sacred feet. Christian blood flows freely while they believe they are the defenders of the church, the bride of Christ, through having routed those they call her foes. As if the deadliest enemies of the church were not these impious pontiffs who devote themselves to war, who allow Christ to be forgotten through their silence, misrepresent him with their forced interpretations of his teaching and slay him with their obnoxious way of life' (pp.136-139).

Folly even found herself well represented in Scripture. 'It is quite clear that the Christian religion has a kind of kinship with folly. Paul attributes folly even to God. He says that "God's foolishness is wiser than men". Christ too was made something of a fool in order to help the folly of mankind when he assumed the nature and form of man, just as he was made sin so that he could redeem sinners. Paul himself said "receive me as a fool". He admitted that "we are fools for Christ's sake", which is a high tribute to folly from a great authority. So we should not be surprised if Festus judged him to be mad' (pp.147-149).

Then Erasmus cut Folly out altogether and spoke directly to the reader himself. 'So we have a situation which I think is not unlike the one in the myth in Plato's *Republic*, where those who were chained in a cave marvelled at shadows, whereas the man who had escaped and then returned to the cavern told them that he had seen real things and they were much mistaken in their belief that nothing existed but their wretched shadows. This man who has gained understanding pities his companions and deplores their insanity, which confines them to such an illusion, but they in their turn laugh at him as if he were crazy and turn him out' (p.150).

This myth of Plato's precisely describes Erasmus' view of the Church on his return from Rome. Using the word 'pious' to denote the true and enlightened Christian, he went straight on to explain his opinion in detail.

'In the same way the common herd of men feels admiration only for the things of the body and believes that these alone exist, whereas the pious scorn whatever concerns the body and are wholly uplifted towards the contemplation of invisible things. The ordinary man gives first place to wealth, the second to bodily comforts, and leaves the last to the soul – which anyway most people believe doesn't exist, because it is invisible to the eye. By contrast, the pious direct their entire endeavour towards God, who is absolute purity, waging unceasing war against lust, anger, pride and envy, while the crowd thinks life impossible without them. The pious say that the ritual with which the Eucharist is celebrated should not be rejected, but in itself it serves no useful purpose. It can be positively harmful if it lacks the spiritual element represented by visible symbols. It represents the death of Christ, which men must express through the mastery and extinction of their bodily passions, laying them in the tomb as it were, in order to rise again to a new life wherein they can be united with him and with each other. This then is how the pious man acts and this is his purpose. The crowd, on the other hand, thinks the sacrifice of the mass means no more than crowding as close as possible to the altars, hearing the sound of the words and watching other small details of the ritual. There is total disagreement between the two parties on every point and each thinks the other mad' (pp.150-152).

Winding up her case Folly asks, 'what will life in heaven

be like?', but when Erasmus replies that 'eye has not seen nor ear heard, nor have entered into the heart of man, the things which God has prepared for those that love him', it suddenly seemed best to stop. 'Those who are granted a foretaste of this, experience something which is very like madness. But I've been forgetting who I am and I've overshot the mark. If anything I have said seems rather impudent, you must remember it is Folly and a woman who has been speaking' (pp.152-3).

It is almost impossible to convey an adequate idea of the complexity of this unique book. Although the arresting title and the liveliness of the writing quickly capture attention, it is littered with allusions to the classics, while the intensity of the author's thinking can at times be baffling. Yet it soon became a best seller. There were forty Latin editions in twenty-five years, as well as several translations. Many people were shocked to realize that Erasmus was such an ecclesiastical rebel.

5

Disappointment and Achievements

Almost an Englishman; New Testament revision; Julius

1509-1514: London, Cambridge

For some time Erasmus remained in London with Thomas More's family, but after Mrs More's death Thomas married an older woman and he no longer felt so welcome in the home. In August 1511 he settled at Queens' College in Cambridge. 'There was nothing to eat the whole journey through: unending rain, thunder and lightning. Three times my horse fell headlong to the ground.' And he soon realised that he had little prospect of earning his living in Cambridge. 'What can I filch from people who haven't a rag to their backs?' (225:4-8, 16-17). When he started lecturing on Greek grammar, few people attended. He contemplated teaching theology, but 'the pay is too small to tempt me' (233:10-15). Although we have thirty-three of his letters from Cambridge, none of them refer to the University or give any clear account of how he spent his time. He avoided travel, 'partly because of the plague, partly because of highway robberies – there is a crop of them in England at present' (282:26-28). 'I have been living a snail's life for several months. Enclosed and bottled up at home, I brood over my studies. Everything is very deserted here, most people being away for fear of the plague, even though when all of them are present it is a lonely place for me. Expenses are impossibly high and not a penny to be made' (282:49-53).

It was a painful contrast to what he had expected. 'It seems to me that I deserve every kind of misfortune whenever I reflect what Italy was, the climate, the libraries, the honeyed talks with scholars, the prospects that I put from me so readily, and how Rome was smiling on me when I left her' (253:8-11). And yet, 'what good does it do to count the waves in one's wake?' (248:28).

Back in London he felt better. 'I have a great many friends: several bishops have shown me exceptional kindness, among them the Archbishop of Canterbury, who treats me with such affection that no brother or even father could be more loving. By his gift I hold a substantial income and further support is given me by the generosity of prominent men, though preparations for war have brought about a sudden change in the character of this island and the price of everything is going up day by day' (288:10-19). King Henry was far too deeply involved in war with France to pay much attention to him. 'How can anything in this world be so important as to impel us to so deadly a thing as war, seeing we boast of naming ourselves after Christ, who preached and practised gentleness? If anything happens to the Roman Church who could more properly be blamed for it than the all-too-mighty Julius, who has succeeded in arousing this hurricane?' (288:38-45, 98-99, 245:23-25).

Notwithstanding his ignorance of the English language

and his general impression that 'among the Britons the avoidance of hard work is so prevalent and the love of ease so great' (292:8-9), he gradually came to feel 'almost entirely transformed into an Englishman' (252:16-17). And in spite of all disappointments and his normal ill-health, his achievements during these years were a remarkable prelude to still greater fame. Even at Cambridge he by no means wasted his time. 'My mind is so excited at the thought of emending Jerome's text', he said at Queens'. 'I have almost finished collating a large number of manuscripts' (273:15-19). He continued to translate dialogues of Lucian, still enjoying his 'civilised laughter' (293:23), and he embarked upon numerous translations into Latin of what he called 'the treasures of Plutarch', for he reckoned that 'even Greece never produced an author to surpass him in learning and style', though distressed that copyists over many centuries had introduced 'monstrous faults at well-nigh every line' (268:12-20 and 284:12-14). The same of course was true of the Bible, and 'the collation of the New Testament', comparing handwritten manuscripts and eliminating errors, was another major task on which he made great progress (270:67). He was also able to complete his *Foundations of the Abundant Style*, begun many years earlier, which proved invaluable to boys studying Latin. John Colet, by this time Dean of St. Paul's, was delighted to have it for St. Paul's School, which he had founded and financed. It was soon in such demand across Europe that 85 editions were published.

On February 20, 1513, three and a half years after Erasmus left Rome, Julius II died at the age of seventy. He had been a most influential Pope, attracting to the capital many talented artists whose achievements adorn it to this day. It was he who took the decision to demolish the original St. Peter's Church which had stood for over a thousand years. And it was he who descended a rope ladder to a great depth to lay the foundation stone of the present St. Peter's. Even Erasmus conceded that 'Julius was a very great man – the fact that he embroiled almost the whole world in war shows that, I grant you' (335:113-114). Shortly after his death an anonymous pamphlet was in circulation which recounted what happened when he arrived at the gate of heaven. The Apostle Peter refused to let him in. Although Julius indignantly stressed his immense services to the Church, Peter with equal determination detailed his wickedness and insisted that 'you can't come in here unless you are holy'. He described the Pope as the enemy of Christ, as Julius Caesar come back from hell in disguise, as the sink of iniquity, wielding satanic power clearly evident in his many vices and crimes, his drunkenness and adulteries, his obsession with money, and the wars he promoted and enjoyed, 'his blood-stained armour' underneath his priestly robes. But while portraying Julius as such a loathsome monster, the booklet spoke warmly of Christ, the true head of the Church, who died to rescue us from vice, enriching us for all eternity, instructing us what to do and what to shun.

Although *Julius Excluded from Heaven* was written in 1513 and even put on the stage in Paris in 1514, it does not seem to have been published till 1517, when it at once became immensely popular. 'Everybody buys it: people talk about nothing else' (849:31-33). It was widely assumed that no one but Erasmus could possibly have written it. A friend of his in Brussels wrote to say, 'How I enjoyed the *Julius*. I paid it the tribute of a continuous chuckle. How delightfully and amusingly, and in a word Erasmically, he argues with Peter' (532:26-28). Yet Erasmus consistently denied that he was the author. 'I am surprised that some people suspect me as the source of this egregious absurdity. I have neither leisure enough to expend an hour of my time on nonsense of this kind, nor a mind so irreligious as to poke fun at the Holy Father, nor am I fool enough to want to unsheathe the pen against those who can reply with the sword' (622:20-22, 636:22-25). Yet Thomas More told him he had seen 'only a first draft and nothing really complete, but in your writing' (502:11-14) and in fact no serious doubt remains that Erasmus was responsible. He admitted that 'people claim as mine books which I never wrote, or at least did not write with a view to publication. Some servant, I suspect, filched them and sold them to the printers' (341:3-12).

In early July 1514 he had decided to leave England, so 'I paid my respects to His Majesty, King Henry VIII, in person', but all he could say was that 'he received me with the friendliest expression'. The Channel crossing went well. The sea was calm and the weather glorious, yet once again Dover treated him harshly. 'The portmanteau crammed with my writings was put on a different boat. They make a habit of doing this deliberately in order to steal something if they can. Believing that several years' work was lost, I was afflicted by a degree of anguish as keen, I think, as any parent would suffer upon the death of his children. I often wonder that such dregs of mankind are tolerated by the English government to the great annoyance of visitors and the discredit of the whole island' (295:6-21).

He felt it necessary to contact the prior of the monastery where he had spent some years in his youth, to explain that he had no intention of returning. 'We make Christianity consist in place, dress, diet, and numbers of petty observances, regarding as a lost soul one who exchanges his white habit for a black one, or his cowl for a cap. So-called religious obligations of this kind have done great harm, even though they may have been first introduced as a result of pious fervour. Later they gradually increased and extended into myriads of distinctions backed up by the authority of the popes, given too readily and indulgently in many cases. Yet in these cold rites men find self-satisfaction and by these they judge and condemn others. How much more consonant with Christ's teaching it would be to regard the entire Christian world as a single household, a single monastery as it were, and to think of all men as one's brethren' (296:75-91). Then he neatly summarised his achievements in England. 'In the last two years I have, among many other things, revised Jerome's epistles and elucidated the obscure parts in my notes. I have also revised the whole of the New Testament from a collation of ancient Greek manuscripts and have annotated over a thousand places. And I have begun a series of commentaries on Paul's epistles, for I have made up my mind to give up my life to sacred literature. At present I am making for Germany, Basel in fact' (296:161-169, 241).

6

A Great Printing Shop

Froben; Jerome; Gillis; *Folly* defended

1514-1515: Basel, London, Antwerp

From Calais he travelled across Belgium to Antwerp, undeterred by 'the extreme peril of the journey' (333:92) or by a painful injury which he suffered 'in the open county, six very long miles from Ghent'. As he bent over to speak to his servant 'my horse was frightened by some linen sheets spread on the ground and shied in the opposite direction, severely twisting the base of my spine. The sudden torment was unbearable. Whatever it was, it was no ordinary affliction, so I stayed in Ghent for several days and there I found the President of Flanders, Jean Le Sauvage, a very well-read man' (301:6-38), who was later to play a significant role in his life.

He then embarked on the long ride up the Rhine, feeling it was essential to meet Johann Froben, the Basel printer, who for his own profit had produced a pirated version of the *Adages* published in Venice. Several other manuscripts of Erasmus, written in England, had also found their way to him. Moreover, Froben was involved in a new edition of Jerome's writings. Erasmus anticipated staying a month in Basel before going on to Rome to bring to birth the major projects he had in mind (300:43).

He recorded nothing about the trip until he reached Strasbourg, where he was rapturously received not only by 'the two distinguished magistrates at the head of the city' but also by 'the literary society of Strasbourg', which included twelve prominent scholars and Matthias Schürer, a printer already producing his books (305:62, 302:1-17). When he got to Sélestat he had to insist on moving on quickly, but Johann Witz, headmaster of a famous school there, went with him to Basel in mid-August. 'I told him not to advertise my arrival, so to begin with I saw no one except the men I really wanted to see.' Froben had never met him, so Erasmus took an unusual decision. 'I gave him a letter from Erasmus, adding that I was very closely acquainted with him, that he had entrusted to me the whole business of publishing his work, in fact I said that Erasmus and I are so alike that if you have seen one you have seen the other. He was delighted later on, when he saw through the trick I had played on him' (305:192-197). And then he met Froben's colleagues, Beatus Rhenanus, son of a butcher at Sélestat, 'that town so fertile in learned and gifted men', whose 'unassuming wisdom and keen literary judgement are a great pleasure to me', and Bruno Amerbach, 'a young man born to be my friend, who has the three tongues, Latin, Greek, and Hebrew'. The rector of Basel University and 'the doctors of all the faculties' invited him to supper the next day, while enthusiastic letters came from Udalricus Zasius 'doctor and professor of law in the University of Freiburg', who addressed him as 'the glory of the world, the shining light of all living men' (303:14-21). To crown the welcome, Froben's father-in-law 'paid off all that was owing in my inn and took me along with horses and baggage to stay in his house'. Erasmus was so 'charmed and attracted by my native Germany that I am ashamed and annoyed to have so long put off getting to know it' (305:146-199).

Although he had expected to go on to Rome in September, Froben soon put a stop to that. In a few weeks Erasmus' translations of Plutarch and a new edition of his *Adages* were in the press, as well as a collection of metaphors, 'many jewels in one small book, selected from the richly furnished world of the greatest authors of antiquity, noted down by the way as I reread Aristotle, Pliny, Plutarch and Seneca. In this field there is a twofold difficulty and double praise is to be won. The first task is to have tracked down what is really good. But it is no less labour to arrange neatly what you have discovered, just as it is something to have found a precious jewel in the first place but there is credit to be won from its skilful mounting in a ring' (312:18-22, 58-63).

As though that were not more than enough, 'There remains the New Testament translated into Latin by me, with the Greek facing and notes on it, as well as the letters of Jerome with the text corrected and also explanatory comments, which keep me so completely tied down that I scarcely have time for meals' (305:228-234, 14-16).

Meanwhile Matthias Schürer, stimulated by having actually met Erasmus face to face, began publishing further editions of the *Foundations of the Abundant Style* in Strasbourg. And an admirer at Tübingen assured him, 'Now that I learn you are busy in the cause of good literature at Basel, I am filled with joy, for, to say exactly what I think, I believe you are the one person to whose gifts all other living men must yield' (321:6-12).

Rather surprisingly, he then left Basel for about four months. On March 1, 1515 he announced, 'I am all packed up and just off to Rome' (324:26-27), but changed his mind and headed for London. From Strasbourg Matthias Schürer travelled with him to Frankfurt after he had lost some of his money in Mainz in spite of concealing it in his leggings for safety (326B:3-10). At Ghent he renewed his earlier contacts and was obliged to stay a few days at Saint Omer when his horses grew weary. Not wanting to waste time, and thinking of Beatus Rhenanus putting the works of Seneca through two printing presses in Basel, he drew up an exposition of Psalm 1, treating it as 'an actual working plan for true beatitude, sketched by the pencil of the Holy Spirit' (327:7-18). It was one of the few occasions when he gave his mind to verses in the Old Testament.

On May 7 he wrote from London, 'The Channel crossing was expensive and dangerous, but rapid. My box has not yet arrived, which is the most unfortunate thing that could have happened to me. All my materials for Jerome are in it and unless I recover them soon, the men who are printing it in Basel will run out of work. If this has happened deliberately it was a most hostile act, for there is no way in which they could have done me more harm. I intended to present the bishops with their copies. As it is, I pay my respects empty-handed and they send me away empty-handed in return' (332:6-15).

Presumably the box arrived safely after all, for on May 21 he wrote a long letter to the new Pope, Leo X, dedicating to him his edition of Jerome's writings – 'This great work is now at press and will run, I think, to ten volumes. I saw clearly enough that Italy would be invaluable for the publication of my work, but in the nick of time I found in

Basel several people who were all set for this task and had in fact already started, especially Johann Froben, whose skill and outlay are a mainstay of the enterprise, and with him three very learned young men, the brothers Amerbach, who seem to have been designed by the Fates themselves expressly so that by their agency Jerome might rise from the dead. Their father, a most excellent man, had taken care to have his three sons taught Greek, Hebrew and Latin. On his deathbed he commended this objective to them, which they have pursued with such energy, sharing Jerome with me on the understanding that everything outside the letters should be their responsibility. One could almost say that I have worked myself to death so that Jerome might live again. A great printing shop is now in full activity' (333:81-88, 334:127-137, 335:329-338).

At Antwerp on his way back to Basel he received a letter from Maarten van Dorp, a professor of philosophy in Belgium, who began by saying, 'We have known each other well for a long time and anything I write, however outspokenly, comes from one who is your devoted friend, eager to preserve your name and fame. I think you ought to know how people feel about you in your absence. And the first thing I must tell you is that *The Praise of Folly* has aroused a good deal of feeling even among your most faithful supporters. Those who approved it at all points were very few indeed. Many people are greatly offended. What good did it do to attack the faculty of theology so bitterly? What gain can there be if people who used to praise you to the skies now eat their words, say hard things about you, accuse you falsely, and turn against you one and all? In the old days everyone admired you, they all read you eagerly, longing to have you here in person, and now this wretched *Folly* has upset everything. Your style, your fancy, your wit they like, your mockery they do not like at all. Those who condemn you and your work are only human, they do it from weakness not wickedness, and they do it for good reason, a reason they have been provided with by you' (304:18-75).

At Antwerp Erasmus was the guest of Pieter Gillis, chief secretary of the town, a close friend for over thirty years. He stayed so often with Pieter and his wife Cornelia that no less than 83 of his surviving letters were written there. Van Dorp's letter had been badly delayed, and 'I still feel the upset of my sea-voyage and the weariness of riding that followed', but he thought it better to answer at once rather than 'leave a friend thinking as you do'. His reply, seven hundred lines of it, was such a brilliant defence of *The Praise of Folly* that for many years it used to be printed along with the book. He confessed that 'to be perfectly frank I am almost sorry myself that I published it', because of the ill-will it had aroused, yet he was not prepared to retract anything he had said. 'My purpose was to show men how to become better, to help, not to hurt. In *The Handbook of the Christian Soldier* I laid down quite simply the pattern of a Christian life and the *Folly* is concerned in a playful spirit with the same subject. Plato criticised many people by name. So did Aristotle, Cicero, and Seneca. Jerome, pious and serious as he was, could not refrain from outbursts of indignation and bitter invective against individuals. In the *Folly* I criticise no one by name. If anyone takes offence he is his own betrayer, having made it plain that a criticism applies to him in particular, for it was levelled at no individual except such as deliberately made the cap fit. You must understand how much I leave unsaid, ashamed to record what many men practise without shame, for some things in human behaviour are too disgusting to be described without embarrassment. Do I ever uncover a sink of iniquity or stir the mud that lurks beneath the life of man? Everyone knows how much may be said against evil popes and selfish bishops. St. Paul says "Rebuke, reprove, exhort, in season, out of season" (2 Tim. 4:2). The apostle thinks faults should be attacked in every possible way, and do you think no sore place should be touched? Do you call it an attack on the faculty of theology if foolish and badly behaved theologians unworthy of the name come in for some criticisms? They find *Folly* intolerable because she discharged a few shafts of wit, not against scholarly theologians, but against the frivolous quibbling of ignorant dolts. In fact I would not approve of *Folly* myself unless such people did disapprove. Why did the Archbishop of Canterbury take no offense? Because he knows none of it applies to him. I have often heard men who are real theologians, upright and scholarly men who have drunk deep of Christ's teaching from the true springs, regret the arrival in the world of this newer kind of theology, so adulterated with Aristotle and trivial human fantasies that I doubt whether any genuine trace of Christ remains. What Christ taught and what mere human traditions ordain are not the same. What have petty arguments to do with the mysteries of eternal wisdom, with the old true Christianity?' (337:1-460).

Throughout this impressive explanation Erasmus repeatedly suggested that 'Because truth is a trifle astringent, a cheerful and humorous style of putting people right is with many of them most successful. The Gospel truth slips into our minds more agreeably and takes root there more decisively when it has charms like Christ's parables to commend it, than if it were produced naked. By conducting all the action through an imaginary comic character I have tried to arrange that even peevish folk may take it in good part. Let any fair-minded man read what I wrote and he will find the allegory acceptable. I should not like to have written even in jest anything that could in any way weaken a Christian's faith, but I must be allowed a reader who understands what I have written and is keen to learn the truth. Even Paul calls Christ sin, calls him an accursed thing. What outrageous impiety, if one chose a malevolent interpretation, but what a tribute if one accepts it as Paul meant it. In his triumph through the cross he robbed hell of its plunder, which he restored to the Father' (337:109-127, 470-473, 598-601, 530-539).

Having justified his technique, Erasmus had advice for van Dorp himself. 'A knowledge of Greek and Hebrew is so important for our understanding of Scripture that I shall not cease to urge you, most excellent Maarten, to add to your equipment at least a knowledge of Greek. You are exceptionally gifted. You can write solid, vigorous, easy, abundant stuff. Your energy is still fresh and green, and you have successfully completed the conventional course of study. Take my word for it, if you crown such a promising start with a knowledge of Greek you will do great things. But if, in the present state of human affairs, you anticipate a true understanding of the science of theology without a knowledge of the language in which most of Scripture has been handed down, you are wholly at sea. If my affection for you carries any weight, if there is anything in our being fellow-countrymen, if my age has any influence with you – for I am old enough to be your father – let me persuade you to agree to this. Otherwise I fear that when you are older and have learnt from experience, you will approve my advice and regret your decision, not understanding your mistake till it is too late to remedy it' (337:636-677).

7

The Greek and Latin New Testaments

Oecolampadius; Zwingli's visit; Pirckheimer

1515-1516: Basel

Maarten van Dorp had something else on his mind as well as *The Praise of Folly*. 'I understand that you have also revised the New Testament and written notes on over a thousand passages. This raises another point on which I should like in the friendliest possible spirit to issue a warning. What sort of operation is this, to correct the Scriptures, and in particular to correct Latin copies by means of the Greek?' He felt it was preposterous to suggest that the Vulgate, the Latin Bible used by the church for eleven hundred years, was full of errors. 'It will do a great deal of harm. Many people will have doubts about the integrity of the Scriptures if the presence of the least scrap of falsehood in them becomes known' (304:90-163).

In his reply Erasmus made no concessions at all. 'I wonder what has beguiled your very clear-sighted mind. You write like one of our ordinary divines who habitually attribute to the authority of the church anything that has somehow slipped into current usage. Supposing some synod has approved the Vulgate, did it approve it in such terms that it is absolutely forbidden to correct it by the

Greek original? Were all the mistakes approved as well?' (377:750-2, 807-814). He explained precisely why the Vulgate needed correction. 'Often through the translator's clumsiness or inattention the Greek has been wrongly rendered, often the true reading has been corrupted by ignorant scribes, for it is of the nature of textual corruption that one error should generate another, and not seldom the text has gone astray entirely.' Prolonged research having convinced him of this, 'I have translated the whole New Testament after comparison with the Greek copies and have added the Greek on the facing page so that anyone may easily compare it. And I have appended separate annotations in which I show that my emendations are not haphazard alterations' (337:768-777 and 905-909). None of this had actually been published yet, which was why he was on his way back to Basel, but he had spoken in similar terms a year before (296:164-166), so it is evident that most of the work had been done in Cambridge and London (264:16, 270:67, 305:13-14). It is necessary to emphasise the immense significance of his achievement. Just as Jerome had translated the entire Old Testament from the original Hebrew into Latin, so Erasmus had translated the entire New Testament from the original Greek into Latin, something Jerome had never done. A distinguished German lawyer in Strasbourg wrote to say, 'I cannot but rejoice that I have lived to see the day when this new sun is about to rise upon the world' (352:15-16).

By mid-July 1515 he was back in Basel. 'The journey was always at risk from robbers, beside which, the Rhine being swollen with snow and rain, everything was under water, so that there was more swimming than riding. But now we have in the press the New Testament in Greek, as it was written by the apostles, and in Latin as translated by me, together with my notes' (348:9-14). These extensive notes were not comments on the gospel message but purely textual, to show why his translations varied from the Vulgate. 'Pointers' he called them, 'partly to explain to the reader's satisfaction why each change was made, or at least to pacify him if he has found something he does not like, partly that it might not be so easy in future for anyone to spoil a second time what had once been restored with such great exertions' (373:49-54). So both his notes and the Greek New Testament, which had never before been printed, were presented in support of his Latin translation, which created such a stir that it was to be reprinted not less than two hundred times.

He was profoundly moved by this prolonged study of the New Testament in the original language, 'thinking out for myself and weighing up the full force and proper sense of every word, even of every Greek letter, for in the very strokes of the letters lie hid great mysteries of divine wisdom. Not a single word uttered by him whom we worship as the Word himself is beneath our notice. Fruit tastes better when you have picked it with your own hands from the mother tree; water is fresher when you draw it as it bubbles up from the actual spring; and in the same way the Scriptures have about them some sort of natural fragrance, breathing something genuine and peculiarly their own when read in the language in which they were first written by some who took them down from those divine lips, and by some who bequeathed them to us under the influence of the Holy Spirit' (337:113-114, 126-127, 179-191).

Then on September 21, 1515 a young German delivered

to Erasmus a letter from Johann Witz, headmaster of the school at Sélestat. 'The man who brings you this letter,' it said, 'deserves the privilege of your acquaintance because of his character and learning. His name is Oecolampadius, from which it is easily seen that he knows some Greek. His knowledge of theology is evident from his habit of writing papers of great erudition. Besides this, he has a knowledge of Hebrew, which is somewhat out of the ordinary' (354:2-10). And so the postman, who was destined to make no minor contribution to the history of the Christian Church in the next fifteen years, joined Froben's staff toiling to get the bilingual New Testament into people's hands all over Europe. Erasmus himself marvelled at them. 'I seem to be living in some delightful precinct – so many good scholars of no ordinary kind. They all know Latin, they all know Greek, most of them know Hebrew too. One is an expert historian, another an expert theologian: one is skilled in mathematics, one a keen antiquary, another a jurist. How rare this is. I certainly have never before had the luck to live in such a gifted company. And how open-hearted they are, how cheerful, how well they get on together. You would say they had only one soul' (391A:10-18).

He did not just watch them do the printing. In his own remarkable way Erasmus went on improving the huge volume, editing and altering day by day, up to the last minute, even as the presses were working at top speed. On March 7, 1516 he announced triumphantly, 'The New Testament is published' (394:38), though he admitted it would be more accurate to say it had been 'rushed into print' (402:3-4). And then, when he had barely recovered from such 'incredible pressure of work', he had a visitor from eastern Switzerland, a young Catholic priest named Ulrich Zwingli, who later wrote to him on April 29, 1516. 'When I think of writing to you Erasmus, best of men, I am frightened by the brilliance of your learning but at the same time encouraged by the charming kindness you showed me when I came to see you at Basel. You may well have wondered why I did not stay at home, as I did not ask for the solution of any very difficult question. It was that spirited energy of yours I was in search of. It was the courtesy of your character and your well-regulated life that I admired to such an extent that, when I read what you write, I seem to hear you speaking and to see the gestures of that small but far from ungraceful figure. You are the favourite companion with whom we must first have some conversation if we are to get off to sleep. I should like you to know that I am far from regretting my journey to visit you. I have made quite a reputation simply by boasting that I have seen Erasmus, the man who has done so much for liberal studies and the mysteries of Holy Scripture and who is so filled with the love of God and men. We are all specially bound to pray that God may preserve him safe and sound so that theology, rescued by him from barbarism, may grow to full maturity and not be deprived of such a parent while still of tender years' (401:3-35). Already profoundly influenced by Erasmus' books, Zwingli pounced upon his Greek New Testament with great delight, thrilled to be studying the actual words the apostle Paul wrote. This so intensified his grasp of the faith that only a few years later he was to become the leader of the Reformation in Zürich.

And that same spring yet another massive enterprise reached its conclusion, a new edition of the corrected works of Jerome. The Amerbach-Froben press had for years been working towards this goal, as had Erasmus himself since his youth. He drew up a magnificent dedication to William Warham, the Archbishop of Canterbury, deploring the fact that 'the slippers of the saints and their drivel-stained napkins we put to our lips, scraps of their tunics we place in bejewelled reliquaries, while their most powerful relics, the books in which we have the best part of them still living and breathing, we abandon to be gnawed by bugs and cockroaches. It is impossible to find any writer of our faith to compare with him, expert in so many languages, completely at home in sacred and profane literature, so perfect in every department of knowledge. Who had the whole of Scripture by heart as he had, drinking it in, pondering upon it? Who breathes the spirit of Christ more vividly? Who ever followed him more exactly in his way of life? A man who possesses Jerome acquires a well-stocked library, a river of gold. After the writings of the evangelists and apostles, there is nothing more deserving of Christian attention' (396:115-153, 384-5, 349). He explained to the Archbishop the enormous task of comparing manuscripts of Jerome's works to correct the mistakes made by ignorant copyists. 'Everything so damaged, mutilated and muddled, that if Jerome himself came to life again he would neither recognise his own work nor understand it. Let me just say one thing, which is bold but true. I believe that the writing of his books cost Jerome less effort than I spent in the restoring of them, and their birth meant fewer nightly vigils for him than their rebirth did for me' (396:233-235, 258-262).

During 1515 Erasmus began corresponding with Willibald Pirckheimer, 'a great man not easily matched' (322:5), town councillor at Nuremberg, 'blessed with the friendship of famous princes in France and Italy as well as Germany' (326A:2-4). Having studied law and Greek in Italy, he too had translated into Latin some writings of Plutarch and Lucian. A married man with five daughters, Pirckheimer felt 'immersed in public business, obliged to follow the noise and bustle of the law and the squabbles of princes, in which even to please God is perhaps impossible' (375:15-19), but Erasmus considered him 'a very rare bird in this age of ours, combining as you do such outstanding scholarship with so splendid a position in the world' (362:7-9). He was grateful to Erasmus 'for not forgetting me when you are so busy. I rejoice that Jerome has at last found someone to restore him to his original purity. Congratulations. Go on as you have begun, my dear Erasmus, and do not hide the light the Creator has given you under a bushel. Your labours will win you the favour of God and of his saints and of the world' (375:12-21). Then another fine Pirckheimer letter crowned what had been achieved in Basel. 'My dearest Erasmus. You have done very great things for us, far more than we had any right to expect, your splendid publication expounding the New Testament. My two sisters have your writings in their hands continually. They are particularly delighted with the New Testament, which appeals greatly to women who are more learned than many men who think they know something. You have protected your name against all the assaults of time and completed a task useful to all Christ's faithful people. Well done, well done indeed. You have achieved a result that has been denied to all men this side of a thousand years. Farewell, light and glory of the human race' (409:2-11, 29-33).

Critical though Erasmus frequently was of monks, they were not all critical of him, as a letter he received in 1516 from a Benedictine community in Bavaria indicated. 'Such a love of your conversation overcame me long ago during our brief association, the only time we ever met, and such a strong attachment left its mark upon me that I could not really control it, even if I wished to. So unique are the learning and the knowledge which abound or rather overflow in you, the most learned man in all Germany, that I confess myself intoxicated with admiration. Nothing is so rooted in my mind, nothing has made so permanent an impression on my heart, as the vivid idea of you. I seem to see you face to face and enjoy your conversation even while my senses are bound in sleep. Nothing is so successful in refreshing my memory of the past and giving me a new understanding and enjoyment of the present as your productions and all your translations, clear as daylight, from the Greek. You are the glory of Germany, its eye, its sun, its shining light' (391:9-23, 29-34, 51-52).

8

A Public Enemy of Christianity

Archbishop of Canterbury; Capito's warning; herculean labours

1516-1517: Antwerp

He was sorry to leave Basel in the spring of 1516. 'I found Upper Germany so attractive in every way. I like the climate and the friendliness of the people.' He was given a moving farewell, numbers of men on horseback escorting him as he rode out of the city. His intention had been to travel north through France, 'but when I saw bands of soldiers everywhere and country people leaving their homes, I thought better of it'. Keeping to the Rhine valley, he attached himself to a large company of Italians in Cologne. 'We were a party of about eighty horsemen, but even so our journey was not free from peril. Heaven be thanked, I got safely to Antwerp on May 30' (412:1-21).

The main reason for the move was that he had been appointed a counsellor to young Prince Charles, who was destined three years later to become Holy Roman Emperor, an honour which entailed no obligations. As he expressed it, 'I have returned to my own country. Prince Charles has invited me most generously with an annual salary' (446:19-26). He also hoped to visit England, relying on the favour of the King, of Cardinal Wolsey, and of the Archbishop of Canterbury, who wrote to him in genuine admiration. 'I count your New Testament worthy of all praise and your work on Jerome too. These will secure you immortal fame, a divine reward in Heaven, and from me whatever I can provide. You have given my name some honourable mention and thereby secured me an eternity denied to many emperors and kings who have entirely lapsed from the memory of man. I do not see what adequate recompense for immortality I can make you. I cannot forget how much you have done for me in every way, when present by your conversation, in absence by your letters, in general by your published works' (425:1-9, 27-30). And John Colet wrote to him from his mother's home in Stepney to make an important suggestion. 'Having given us the New Testament in better Latin, you should go on to elucidate it with your explanations. If you make the meaning clear, which no one will do better than you, you will confer a great benefit on us all' (423:42-48).

Quickly settling into his new base at Pieter Gillis' home in Antwerp while Froben printed his booklet on the education of a prince, intended for Prince Charles, he switched over to translate a Greek Grammar into Latin, correcting and improving it as he did so in order to attract students by its 'clarity, order, and simplicity'. While his friends were astonished at the fertility of his intellect, what astonished Erasmus was that people should take offense at Greek Grammar, finding it so tedious and unattractive that 'they reject the studies which might bring them much profit for the rest of their lives' (428:1-21).

He spent five weeks in England to renew his friendship with prominent men who helped to support him, but he

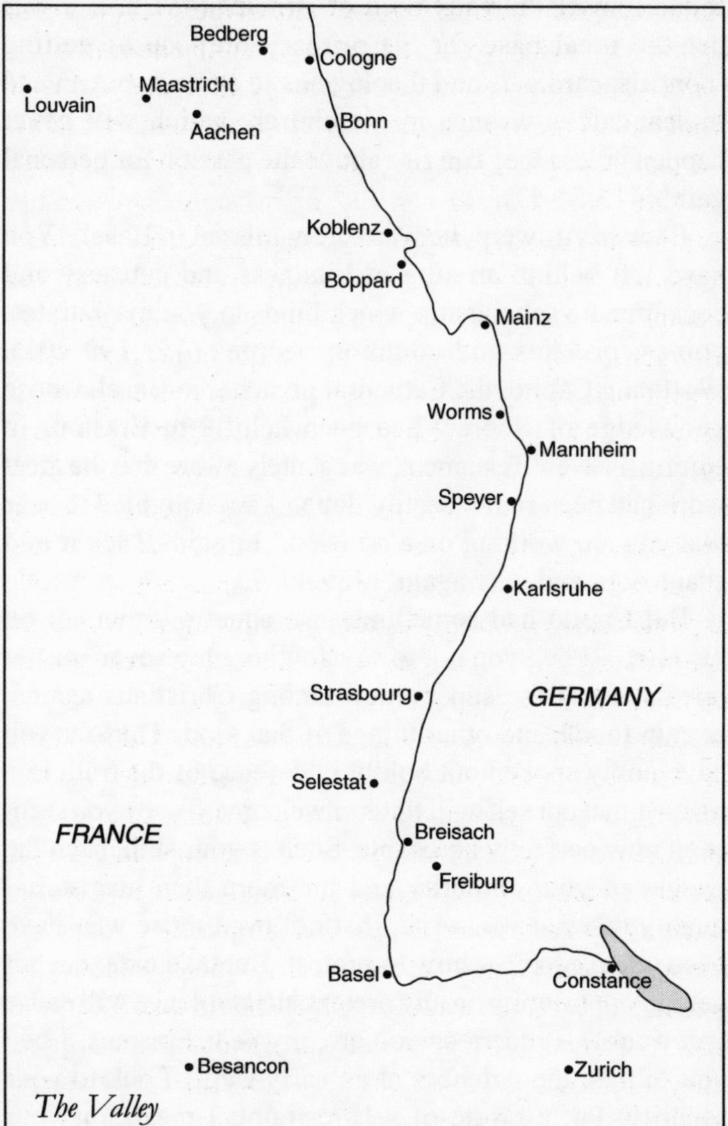

The Valley of the Rhine

found himself 'already tired of Britain' (451:22). It was not the ideal base for his primary purpose of getting 'pontiffs, cardinals and theologians to agree to put an end to scandalous wrongs in the church, which will never happen unless they can rise above the passion for personal gain' (413:54-57).

Back in Antwerp, he was sorely missed in Basel. 'You have left behind an aura of kindness and courtesy and consummate scholarship which binds to you magistrates, nobles, prelates and common people' (459:199-201). Wolfgang Capito, the Cathedral preacher in Basel, whose knowledge of Hebrew had been helpful to Erasmus in editing the New Testament, was acutely aware that the great work had been rather hastily done. 'I am delighted to hear that you are working on a revision,' he said. 'Lick it into shape over and over again' (459:49, 75).

But Capito had something else equally important on his mind. 'I beg you not to say anything too severe or too openly about the superstition among Christians against certain foods, and other things of that kind. Thus far you have nobly spoken out boldly in defence of the truth in a manner that our self-will finds unwelcome. To me you seem even now perfectly agreeable. Such is your skill, such the weight of your authority and the more than magisterial quality of what you write, that not even those who have been attacked know how to protest. But take care: once it gets an opportunity on any pretext, malevolence will cause you trouble. Prudent as you are, my dear Erasmus, I beg you to man the defences at an early stage. Look to your security. Put a bridle of self-restraint, I mean, on your eloquence. You know the current errors in religious practices and doctrine: on penance, on the sacraments, on the superstitions and petty rules of monks or the widespread misunderstandings about the saints, on forced interpretations of Scripture. On all this, say not a word more, unless it is hedged about with your wonderful gift of indirect expression. Once give it an entrance, and the poison of malevolence will force its way into the heart of things. Then they will denounce the name of Erasmus, however truly Christian, as a public enemy of Christianity. It cannot escape you how much people, whose murky acts are shown up by your brilliance, wish to blacken your fairness of mind. So I would wish to see your more outspoken remarks modified, softened by your artistic skill. If, however, you do not feel free to do away with what you have said, at least do not add to it. I have extinguished the rising of passion in many men' (459:83-123).

Then Thomas More had alarming news from London to reveal. 'The bishop is delighted with your version of the New Testament, but there are other people who have formed a conspiracy to read what you write in a very different frame of mind. This horrible plan of theirs gives me some concern, for these men are very sharp. Do not be in a hurry to publish. As for what you have published already, since it is too late for second thoughts, I would urge you to lose no time in going through and correcting everything so as to leave the least possible scope for misrepresentation. Who may they be, you ask? I am quite afraid to name them, for fear your heart sinks in terror before such formidable adversaries. They have divided your works among them and taken an oath that they will read right through everything. You see the peril that hangs over you. You must mobilize all your resources to deal with so great a danger' (481:22-52).

In October 1516 Erasmus was unexpectedly summoned to Brussels by Prince Charles' chancellor, Jean Le Sauvage, whom he had first met at Ghent, 'who in practice is the prince'. It had actually been proposed that he should be sent to Sicily as a bishop. Happily no more was heard of the idea. But he had to get a room near the Court for the winter, which meant leaving Pieter Gillis' home in Antwerp. 'I am most happy to have relieved you of such a burden,' he wrote, 'for I was already developing sympathy for you and your dear wife', but then he proceeded to give Pieter some invaluable advice. 'Good health is mainly in your own hands. Most of our ailments take their rise in the mind. Lay down for yourself some definite course of life, deciding what you wish to do at what time of day. Do not pile one task upon another until the earlier one is finished. Take in hand one good book at a time and do not abandon it until you have finished it. You may find it useful to set up a journal for each year and enter in it briefly day by day anything that happens which you would not wish to forget: it does not take much trouble. Above all I urge you to learn in the conduct of business to follow judgment rather than impulse. If you have too little concern for yourself, mind you do not prove the undoing of someone else as well. A truly great spirit should overlook some wrongs done to it. Give your wife cause to love you and respect you. Let the regular running of your household be sweetened by courtesy and kindness' (476:34-90).

A schoolmaster in the Netherlands revealed the profound influence Erasmus was having on intelligent men across the continent. 'All scholars and true Christians here are devoted to you. The New Testament with your explanations is read eagerly in Greek, even by the aged. Your Herculean labours have laid not merely this present generation but all posterity under a debt. So many people have been won over and inspired by what you write and are now devoted to the study of Scripture and the Christian way of life. Among these, you have certainly won me for Christ. The business of the school distracts me so much, but whenever I am able to steal any time it is all spent reading the Gospels and Paul's Epistles. It is strange yet perfectly true that not a night passes without my finding myself in your company. If I may even tell you my dreams, all last night we were together in Basel, so deeply are you implanted in my heart. Stand your ground and give thanks to God, undeterred by the jealousy, rage and calumny of your critics, a thing you share with Jerome, with Paul, and with Christ Himself' (495:40-52, 500:12-32, 504:31).

In February 1517 he returned to Antwerp, resisting suggestions by the King of France that he settle in Paris. In spite of the warnings he had received he was encouraged by what his writings had achieved. 'Theology has hitherto been taught as a rule by obstinate opponents of the classics, who defend their own ignorance under the cloak of piety. But I am confident of success as soon as the knowledge of Latin, Greek and Hebrew secures public recognition in the universities, as it has already begun to do. Not that I would wish to see the kind of theology which today is established entirely abolished. I want it to be enriched and made more accurate by the incorporation of ancient texts, some things better understood on which the majority of teachers hitherto were deluded. There is still one misgiving in my mind, that under cover of the reborn literature of antiquity paganism may try to rear its ugly head, for we know that even among Christians some scarcely acknowledge Christ in more than name and under the surface are rank heathens; or that the rebirth of Hebrew studies may give Judaism its cue to plan a revival, the bitterest enemy one can find to the teaching of Christ. I could wish that Christ pure and simple might be planted deep into the minds of men and I think this could best be brought about if, aided by the support of the three tongues, we drew our philosophy from the true sources' (541:66-78, 132-138, 149-161).

A lawyer he had never met, a friend of Pirckheimer, wrote to him eagerly from Dresden. 'Greetings Erasmus, chosen vessel and next after Paul as teacher of the Gentiles. I revere your publications like something straight from heaven. May the God of heaven and earth, who has filled you with the spirit of wisdom and understanding, preserve you for the resurrection of ancient Christianity and the ruin of your detractors who, like wolves in sheeps' clothing, assault Christ's fold' (553:2-4, 19-23). And in Paris the greatest of contemporary French intellectuals, Guillaume Budé, shared this elation. 'When I read what Erasmus has published on the New Testament, with immense labour elucidating and virtually resurrecting it, then I feel how fortunate is this age of ours and our successors to have that sacred body of doctrine – the source of our rule of living and dying – rightly ordered and indeed restored to us' (583: 242-249).

Admitting that 'I really hate that Channel crossing' (552:8), he paid a last brief visit to England in April 1517. 'As my companion on the journey by land and sea I took with me a biography of Alexander the Great, which I read as a boy long ago and thought wonderfully clear and terse, rereading it to clear away the rust that has gathered on my Latin and to correct the poverty of my style' (704:16-20).

His return to France was hazardous. 'On the first of May with the wind increasing and by now actually against us, I was roughly put ashore from a ship's boat in the middle of the night, not without peril, under some cliffs on the French coast not far from Boulogne' (584:2-4). Happily he survived, and during the next two months in Antwerp completed one of his most important books, the *Paraphrase of Paul's Epistle to the Romans*.

9

The Paraphrase of the Epistle to the Romans

A running commentary; God's will and man's will

1517: Antwerp

After devoting so many years to the Greek text of the New Testament and producing an accurate version of it in Latin, Erasmus now considered one of Paul's Epistles in a different way. 'In a version the sense is rendered literally. In a paraphrase it is legitimate to add something of your own as well, that may make the author's meaning clearer. For a paraphrase is not a translation but something looser, a kind of continuous commentary, in which the writer and his author retain separate roles' (1274:38-43). He wanted it clearly understood that 'my purpose in writing a paraphrase is not to strike the gospel out of men's hands, but to make it possible for it to be read more conveniently and with greater profit' (1381:444-446). In an age when most Christians did not possess a Bible of their own, when the laity were not encouraged to read it, and when there were still no chapter and verse divisions to make it easier, a lively paraphrase of one book by an acknowledged expert was very attractive. Erasmus admitted what a tremendous struggle he had had 'bridging gaps, smoothing rough passages, bringing order out of confusion and simplicity out of complication, untying knots, throwing light on dark places, and giving Hebrew turns of speech a Roman dress, saying things differently without saying different things' (710:30-36). The outcome is about four times as long as Paul's Epistle. In the New International Version, for example, Romans 5:1-2 reads, 'Since we have been justified through faith we have peace with God through our Lord Jesus Christ, through whom we have gained access by faith into this grace in which we now stand and rejoice in hope of the glory of God'. Part of Erasmus' paraphrase of these words is: 'Since sins alone produce enmity between God and men, now that we who were sinful have been made righteous, we have made our peace with God the Father not through the Mosaic Law nor by the merit of our deeds, but by our faith. And this has come about through the only Son of God, our Lord Jesus Christ, who by washing away our sins with his blood and death, and reconciling God who was previously hostile to us because of our sins, has opened an approach for us so that through the intervention of faith we might be led to this grace of the gospel. In this faith we stand firm, eager and resolute. We even boast that we have a most certain hope spread before us, that through the perseverance of faith we will enjoy at last the glory of God.' Every word is carefully chosen. He stresses 'sins' in the plural, he interprets justified as 'made righteous', and he introduces forgiveness thanks to the 'blood' of Christ. He says Christ reconciled God to us, not us to God. He defines faith as an 'intervention' which must lead to 'perseverance'. And Christian hope is 'most certain'.

Erasmus rarely refers to Adam, so it is instructive to observe how he elaborated on Romans 5:12 and 15, 'Just as sin entered the world through one man and death through sin, and in this way death came to all men because all sinned, how much more did God's grace and the gift that came by Jesus Christ overflow to the many'. The paraphrase reads: 'It was provided by the wonderful and secret plan of God that the way by which our well-being was restored would correspond to the way in which we had suffered ruin. Accordingly, through Adam alone, who first transgressed the law of God, sin crept into the world, dragging along with it death as its companion – the death of the soul, which is the truest form of death – inasmuch as sin is the poison of the soul. And so it happened that the evil originated by the first of the race spread through all posterity, since no one fails to imitate the example of the first parent. Just as sin originated through one man, so through the one Christ, in whom we are all born again through faith, innocence has been introduced along with life, its companion, and this felicity flows down to all who belong to Christ by faith and who eagerly follow him by a blameless life.'

Living in so many different places and having no responsibilities in any particular congregation, preaching was not part of Erasmus' work. 'I have preached before now, but I think that I make better use of my time by writing books' (1162:71-74). He described his paraphrase as a sort of running commentary, but it often became a sermon too, particularly in expanding such a text as Romans 12:1-2. 'Now that by the gift of God you have been brought over from your former superstition to the true religion,' he said, 'henceforth sacrifice to him victims worthy of this profession, not goats or sheep or oxen, for this custom belongs to the heathen and the Jews. God requires from you another kind of worship. You should offer your own bodies, a living sacrifice, a rational sacrifice, in which the mind is the victim. Sacrifice your disposition to pride rather than a calf, your boiling anger instead of a ram, your lust instead of a goat, the seductive thoughts of your mind instead of pigeons and doves. These are the sacrifices worthy of a Christian. God is spirit and he demands to be worshipped not by ceremonies but by pure affections. Instead of circumcision, cut away from your heart superfluous and unbecoming desires. Let the sabbath be for you a mind free from the tumult of disturbing passions. Christ has offered himself for us: it is right that we in turn should sacrifice ourselves for him. And so it will come about that you will be transformed into new persons, into heavenly creatures as far as possible, if not yet by the immortality of the body then certainly by a new state of mind, henceforth taking no pleasure in what is approved by the vulgar crowd.'

Yet nothing Erasmus wrote in this paraphrase was to attract greater attention than his treatment of the statement in Romans 9:18 that 'God has mercy on whom He wants to have mercy and He hardens whom he wants to harden'. He explained, 'it is not by willing or by exertion that salvation is attained, but by the mercy of God.' Then he faced the problem directly. 'We desire in vain and we strive in vain, unless a willing God draws us to Him. Moreover, He draws to himself whoever He chooses, even those who have merited nothing, and He rejects those who are guilty of nothing. However, it does not follow that God is unjust to anyone, but that he is merciful to many. No one is condemned except by his own guilt. No on is saved except by the kindness of God. For God does not harden human minds to hinder them from believing in the gospel of Christ, but He uses the stubbornness of those who refuse to believe to illuminate the magnitude of his kindness. He did not harden the heart of Pharaoh in such a way that He himself caused Pharaoh's stubbornness, but little by little used heavier punishments against him, by which Pharaoh might have been corrected if he had not resisted by his own ill will. The will of God is not the cause of your destruction.'

In years to come it was pointed out to Erasmus that 'those who disapprove of your recognition of free will protest that you have turned Paul's words and intention upside down' (1265:12-16), for the ninth chapter of the Epistle certainly contains no such recognition. But he maintained that since he was writing a paraphrase, not a translation, it was legitimate to balance what Paul said in Romans 9 with what was frequently stated and implied throughout the New Testament. 'I controlled my language so as to allot a very small share to freedom of the will for fear of encouraging such a mortal form of sloth, which consists in everybody abandoning all efforts towards an improvement of life, since what God has once decided is sure to happen. Philosophers were disputing about fate before the birth of Christ and from them there have descended to us these insoluble problems about foreknowledge, about predestination by God, about human free will, in which I think it best not to spend too much anxious time, since this is an abyss no man can get to the bottom of. I would rather teach the doctrines that encourage us to try for the best in every way we can, while yet at the same time claiming no credit for ourselves but leaving the judgment of everything to God' (1342:1056-1078).

To Erasmus' delight the *Paraphrase of Romans* 'was received with applause in learned circles, praised by everyone' (835:4, 794:87). A year after it was published he could confess, 'It is pure bliss to win great gratitude for small pains. Writing a paraphrase is child's play compared with the efforts which the New Testament cost me. That everyone should find Paul more attractive will be quite sufficient return for all my labours. It must, I think, have been a success, to judge by the frequent reprints' (962:4-10, 1017:3-4). Dozens of editions and several translations followed. One very important result was that he decided to produce paraphrases of Paul's other epistles in the next few years.

10

The Slave of the New Testament

Luther's Theses; Lefèvre's criticisms; the Trilingual College

1517-1518: Louvain

By July 10, 1517 he had left Antwerp for the university city of Louvain, ten miles east of Brussels. 'My fortunes carry me now this way and now that, but it seems that Louvain is to be my headquarters, where I keep my library. Between me and the theologians there is a surprising degree of intimacy: I find them fair-minded and friendly. I have been co-opted a member of the faculty of theology, although I am not a doctor of this university' (605:9-11, 794:34, 694:4-16).

For the rest of 1517, while his paraphrase of Romans was being printed, he was absorbed in the revision of his own Latin New Testament. He told Cardinal Wolsey, 'I am the slave of the New Testament so completely that I can do nothing else' (658:40). The task proved more arduous than compiling the paraphrase. 'What I rushed into print rather than edited in Basel is now being taken to pieces and refashioned so thoroughly that it will be a new book. I rescue the Testament from senility and myself grow old.

While I restore it to its original splendour, I cover myself with dust and cobwebs, for toil of this kind brings very little pleasure but much tedium and nuisance' (694:9-10; 745:30-36). He felt he was struggling through a pitch-dark tunnel in a huge mountain range, thankful for a spot of light in the distance which promised an eventual way out. He feared that his eyesight and even the vigour of his mind might be damaged. 'This winter has seemed longer than a hundred years' (761:10). Yet he knew he must go on to the very end, convinced that what he was doing would be invaluable to many people. 'Perhaps I was born for this, with the approval as I hope of Christ, for to please him alone is quite enough. My health is such that I can hardly keep well, pottering up and down in front of a bright fire, buried in my nest like a cuckoo' (758:16, 756:14-16). Meanwhile, all unknown to him, on October 31 a professor of theology named Martin Luther had nailed his ninety-five Theses to the door of the Castle Church in faraway Wittenberg.

Achieving so much under such intense strain, it is hardly surprising that Erasmus was also severely tempted during those days, disappointing many admirers by revealing his human perversity and fallibility. 'I for the present follow Christ, but afar off, as Peter did in his time of weakness; yet it is something to follow him even at a distance; Peter found the profit of it and I hope it will profit me too, if only Jesus in his goodness and mercy will deign to turn his eyes upon me' (605:12-16). He fell out with his friend Jacques Lefèvre d'Etaples, the brilliant scholar who was later to publish the first French New Testament. Lefèvre had criticised Erasmus' notes on the second chapter of the Epistle to the Hebrews. 'Not satisfied with maintaining his own interpretation, he attacks mine in a rather unpleasant way, representing me as degrading the glory of Christ, siding with blasphemous Jews, and saying things unworthy of Christ and of God. I am willing to learn and to be told I am wrong, but I will not put up with being accused of impiety towards Christ' (607:7-8, 784:29-31, 724:10-12). With his customary genius he contrived in a mere two weeks to draw up a formidable defence of himself, denouncing Lefèvre's charges. It was soon on sale all over the continent. When Thomas More read it, his quick response was 'never did I perceive your eloquence more clearly or admire it less' (683:36). A learned physician in Lyon wrote anxiously to both Erasmus and Lefèvre, 'I am distressed to see two of the leading lights of the whole world fighting so fiercely on a small matter, a question of almost no importance', for the crux of the issue was the meaning of a word from Psalm 8 quoted in Hebrews 2:7 (680A:16-20). But Erasmus was undeterred, even though Lefèvre took no part in the controversy beyond the original criticism in one of his books. He kept speaking against Lefèvre in his wide correspondence and he brought out three further editions of his defence. In the end it was Guillaume Budé in Paris who gave him the advice he badly needed. 'There you are with all that reputation, all that glory earned by such a list of publications, raised to such a pinnacle of distinction by all your achievements, and yet in controversies like this you put your trust more in disputatiousness and dreary pamphlets. It seems to me that you would be victorious all the sooner if you stood your ground in silence and refused to listen to attacks on what you have written, rather than treating the charges as though they deserved serious attention. If you add one word more, your friends will never forgive you. Do not think I am arguing on Lefèvre's side. It is you I am sorry for, when I urge you to resume your own proper nature, to return to yourself and to us, and give yourself once again to sacred study and research' (810:114-117, 330-334).

It must also be admitted that during the last months of 1517 Erasmus wrote most uncharacteristically about a Jew who had become a Dominican friar and then published a book against the great Hebrew scholar Reuchlin, whom Erasmus was eager to defend. It is distressing to read the ferocious and abusive language in which he spoke of this man, so contrary to his normal convictions about the meekness and gentleness of Christ. He rashly referred to Satan as 'the friend of the Jews' (703:22-23), yet at the same time he could joyfully report that 'a man has recently arrived here, by race a Jew but in religion a Christian of long standing and by profession a physician, so skilled in the whole of Hebrew literature that in my opinion our age has no one else who could be compared with him' (686:7-10). The special significance of this was that a wealthy friend of Erasmus had died in August, leaving a substantial legacy 'to found a college at Louvain for instruction in the three tongues, Latin, Greek, and Hebrew' (689:15-16). It was ideal that such a competent Hebrew professor should promptly be available. Erasmus hoped he could at once be given a salary since, as he expressed it, 'some favouring deity has offered him to us' (686:19). For the next few years the promotion of the Trilingual College was to be one of Erasmus' main concerns. He was anxious that the Greek professor should be 'a native Greek, from whom his audience could acquire the true pronunciation of Greek at first hand' (836:11-12).

He was rather troubled at the time by Pieter Gillis' distress at his father's terminal illness. 'I beg you to bear with reason what cannot be altered and not to let yourself be overcome with grief which will destroy you. Keep yourself going in your own interest, keep yourself for the benefit of your family, keep yourself for better things to come' (708:2-7). But he was himself taken to task by the famous theologian, Johann Eck, for having said that the apostles learnt Greek from the conversation of ordinary men. 'To write like this is less than prudent of you as a Christian. It was not from the Greeks but by the gift of the Holy Spirit on the day of Pentecost that they learnt their Greek' (769:72-81). Eck had other strong criticisms to make, but for several months Erasmus did not reply.

Though for a time he considered getting his revised New Testament printed by the Aldine Press in Venice –'a complicated business which cannot be done successfully unless I am there to watch over it' – he finally decided to go back to Basel. Froben was delighted, 'but I have nearly four hundred copies of the earlier edition to be sold somehow in the mean time' (801:13). Erasmus told John Colet he was 'setting off on a highly dangerous journey in an age like ours, the most lawless for many centuries, with robberies everywhere. If I am so lucky as to return, I have decided to spend the remainder of my life with you. This will be my retreat from the corruption of the whole world. The Roman curia has abandoned any sense of shame. What could be more shameless than these constant indulgences?' (829:9 and 786:18-26).

11

The Philosophy of Christ

Eck's criticisms; Zasius; monasticism; plague

1518: Basel

On May 13, 1518 Erasmus arrived safely in Basel, suffering from nothing worse than the spring heat. On May 15 he at once sat down to answer Eck's criticisms about mistakes in the Gospels, about how the apostles learnt Greek, and about his preference for Jerome over Augustine.

'In my view the whole of Scripture would not be instantly imperilled, as you suggest, if one of the evangelists by a slip of memory did put one name for another, Isaiah for instance instead of Jeremiah, for this is not a point on which anything turns. The Holy Spirit was present in them as far as pertained to the business of the Gospel, but with this limitation, that in other respects he allowed them to be human none the less. I say this not because I think that the apostles ever did make mistakes, but because I deny that the presence of some mistake must needs shake the credit of the whole of Scripture' (844:36-39, 50-54).

'I do not deny the gift of tongues to the apostles on the day of Pentecost, but it does not follow that they could not have learnt their Greek from ordinary speech. Thanks to the victories of Alexander and the Roman Empire, Egypt and almost the whole of the East spoke Greek. I do not suppose that the Holy Spirit drowned in oblivion what they had previously learnt. We are not told that the apostles spoke Greek by some miracle: we are told that they spoke in some one language, if I mistake not, and were understood by everyone. We read that it happened to them only once' (844:66-87).

'You disapprove of my preference for Jerome over Augustine. It was Augustine I read first and now reread daily as often as need arises, a saintly man endowed with exceptional gifts, but the more I read him the more I feel satisfied with my estimate of the two of them. Let us stick to the facts. No one will deny what great importance lies in birthplace and education. Jerome was born in Stridon, a town so close to Italy, and educated in Rome under the best scholars of the day. Augustine was born in Africa, a barbarous region where literary studies were at an amazingly low ebb. Jerome imbibed the philosophy of Christ with his mother's milk: Augustine was already nearly thirty when he read the Pauline Epistles. Jerome, with all his abilities, devoted 35 years to the study of Holy Scripture: Augustine was diverted at once to the duties of a bishop and compelled to teach what he had not yet learnt. How much better equipped was Jerome, unless perhaps you regard a good knowledge of Greek and Hebrew as of little moment. Augustine acquired only a smattering of Greek, but what book was there in the whole of Greek literature which Jerome did not have at his fingertips? All the same, my love of Augustine is great enough for me to have attempted, in an edition of his works, to do for him what I did for Jerome' (844:205-207, 218-237, 253, 275).

Udalricus Zasius, professor of civil law at Freiburg,

came over to Basel specially to meet Erasmus. 'I wanted to see you at all costs, for since the days of Cicero no age has known a greater scholar or anyone who could surpass you in divine and human learning and in gifts of style. At first sight the authority in your face and glance, and a certain look of the great man, so frightened me that, though I had given much thought beforehand to my reception of you, when I found myself in your presence I could hardly open my mouth to utter a few broken syllables. I guessed this would happen, but even if my reputation suffered for it, I set a high value on meeting you in person. Your measured movements, your easy flow of words like some delighted stream that runs from a fresh spring, your wonderful kindliness, your air of authority graced with a beautiful courtesy – who would not wish to see and wonder at and enjoy all this, even if it cost him something' (857:12-31). He did not need to feel that 'this first interview was a failure', for Erasmus' account of it has also survived. 'I was expecting a lawyer and no more – distinguished, admirable, but still a lawyer. Yet you have pondered the mysteries of theology and you are so much at home in philosophy that it might seem to be your only study. I was not expecting such intellectual vigour in a man of your grey hairs' (859:21-35).

Meanwhile Froben was not only printing the revised Latin New Testament but also an improved edition of *The Handbook of the Christian Soldier* along with Erasmus' new preface dated August 14, 1518, in which he elaborated on the philosophy of Christ, by which expression he simply meant the entire Christian message, the whole gospel, including Christ's teaching as well as 'the divine philosophy of the cross' (1253:22), all of it 'enshrined in the books of the evangelists and apostles' (858:144-146).

'When you are blessed with leisure,' he advised Eck, 'ponder the secrets of the philosophy of Christ in your heart' (844:308-9). Convinced that 'the good life is everybody's business', he wanted the way to it made clear to 'the unlettered multitude for whom Christ died' (858:68, 73).

'When all is dark, when the world is in tumult and men's opinions differ so widely, where can we take refuge if not in the gospel teaching? This generation is the most corrupt there has ever been. When did tyranny and greed lord it so widely and go unpunished? When was so much importance ever attached to ceremonies? When did iniquity abound with so little to restrain it? Our plight would indeed be sorry if Christ had not left us live coals of his teaching. We must blow up those coals into flame. The winter of our wickedness never brings the fire of love so low that it cannot be rekindled. Christ is like a source of eternal fire'(858:173-190, 259).

'At this moment we are preparing to fight the Turks. If, when we have beaten them, they learn how immoral, greedy, profligate, and cruel we are, how can we urge upon them Christ's teaching, which is so entirely different? We shall have found the most effective way of defeating them once they have seen Christ's teaching shining forth in us and realize that we seek nothing but their salvation and the glory of Christ. In my opinion we should seek to win them by entrusting to a number of both saintly and scholarly men the task of reducing into brief compass the whole philosophy of Christ. What concerns the faith should be set out clause by clause, as few as possible. What relates to life should also be imparted in a few words to make them understand that Christ's yoke is good, not harsh. A most merciful Saviour demands nothing from us except a pure and simple life. It is possible they may be won over by kindness: they are human beings as we are: and the most effective thing of all is Christian truth' (858:105-162).

Yet again he expressed his grave misgivings about the monastic system. 'The world is full of monasteries, few of which have any tincture of true religion beyond liturgy and ceremonies' (749:31-33). He admitted that at its beginnings the monastic life had provided a refuge from persecution and constituted 'a summons back to Christ' but then gradually, with the passage of time, 'wealth grew and with wealth ceremonies'. Both piety and simplicity declined. 'And now we see monasteries everywhere whose ways have sunk lower than the laity. Monks who live in leisure and are fed by the liberality of other people, spend all their time in worldly business and exercise a kind of despotism in human affairs, yet because of their dress or some name they bear, they claim so much sanctity that they think other people hardly Christians. Of wicked monks I say nothing for the present' (858:539-599).

He was dangerously ill in Basel in August 1518, suffering from diarrhoea and abdominal pain. 'Things came to such a head that I considered making my will. And now the plague spreading everywhere drives me away from here with the work not yet finished.' On September 3 he boarded a boat heading north down the Rhine for the trip back to Belgium, which was to take him nearly three weeks and almost cost him his life. 'We dined at Breisach and never have I had a more unpleasant meal. The stench was terrible, the flies worse than the stench. Nothing was set on the table that one could possibly eat: dirty porridge, revolting lumps of meat. At nightfall we were put ashore at some dreary village and had supper in a room of no great size, more than sixty of us I should think, the dregs of the human race. In the morning, when it was still quite dark, the boatmen's shouts aroused us. Supperless and sleepless I went on board.' From Strasbourg he travelled on horseback to Speyer, then by carriage to Worms and Mainz, then by boat again to Koblenz.

'When we put in at Boppard and while the boat was being examined, I was stretching my legs on the bank when someone recognised me and pointed me out to the customs officer, whose name was Christoph. I cannot tell you how delighted he was. He carried me off to his house. On his desk, all among the customs forms, lay the works of Erasmus. He cried out at his good fortune, called for his children, his wife, and all his friends. Meanwhile, as the boatmen were protesting loudly, he sent them two flagons of wine, and when there were more protests replied with two more, promising that those who had brought him such a guest would be excused the toll on their return. The wine went down so well with the captain's wife, a great boozer, that she would let no one else have a turn. Before long she was up in arms and nearly killed the cook-maid with her great basting-spoons. Then she emerged onto the upper deck and went for her husband; there was some risk that she would send him headlong out of the boat into the Rhine' (867:50-60, 879:12-19).

Early one Sunday morning they got to Cologne. 'I heard mass.' Then for several hours he rode a lame horse to Bedburg. 'There I spent five delightful days in such tranquillity and comfort that I finished a good part of my revision, for I had brought some of the New Testament with me. But how sudden are the changes in human affairs.

From all these dreams of felicity I was plunged headlong into utter disaster.'

There was still eighty miles to go to Louvain. On a day of violent wind and heavy rain, 'I reached Aachen exhausted by the shaking of the carriage on the rocky road'. Diarrhoea and stomach pains plagued him. 'The fear of robbers was driven out by the distress of my illness.' He began to get boils, large sores, swellings and lumps all over his body as he rode to Maastricht. 'Lack of food and physical effort sapped all my strength. I could take only a little broth. Then my largest boil burst.' For the last six miles 'I found by chance a four-horse carriage and flung myself into it. The discomfort of the going was beyond belief, all the same at 7 o'clock that evening we reached Louvain. I took refuge with Dirk Martens, such a good friend that I could be happy with him' (867:70-210).

'Next day I sent for a surgeon. By now I had acquired a third sore place on my back, caused when my servant massaged me for pain in my kidneys, rubbing too hard with his horny finger. A lump also swelled up on my chest. As the surgeon went away he told Dirk in confidence that it was the plague and he would not come again; but he sent his father, who examined me and assured me to my face that it was a genuine case of plague. I laughed heartily and no idea of plague entered my head for a moment. I sent my water to the physicians, who said there was no sign of disease.' A Jewish doctor agreed. But another much respected physician was so alarmed at Erasmus' sores that he feared the worst. 'I lost patience with physicians and commended my fate to Christ, the great physician. In a couple of days my stomach recovered on minced chicken and a bottle of Burgundy wine, so I went back to work without delay and finished the missing parts of the New Testament. Seventeen days later black dead flesh came away from my sores, though a swelling in my groin seriously frightened me. My recovery in Dirk's house lasted four weeks, then I went back to my own rooms. Only once did I get out to mass, for my strength was not really up to it yet. If it was indeed plague, I drove the plague away at the cost of great effort and discomfort and determination, for often a great part of any disease is our fancy that we have it. Three friends who came every day did away a good part of my illness by their most charming company. Even at the moment when sickness lay most heavy upon me, I was neither tormented by the desire to live nor terrified by fear of death. In Christ alone was all my hope. All I asked of him was that he should give me what he might think best for me' (867:210-290).

12

Shepherds Who Become Wolves

Luther; Corinthian paraphrases; Justus Jonas

1518-1519: Louvain

For the next three years he remained at Louvain. In spite of 'being in poor health and almost done for by the endless toil of writing' (875:5), he poured out a succession of inspiring letters in October 1518.

To the stranger who had welcomed him so eagerly at Boppard he deplored the fact that 'priests and monks should live for their stomach's sake in luxury and ease, while customs officers enter the kingdom of heaven and pursue good literature' (879:2-8). They remained friends throughout life. To the Archbishop of Canterbury he confessed that 'around Aachen I found myself in such torment that I sometimes thought of throwing myself on the ground and just dying there under the open sky' (893:11-14). To John Colet he dared to say, 'What a topsy-turvy world we live in. Out of men we make gods and turn priesthood into tyranny. The princes, together with the pope, are in league against the well-being of the common people. Christ is out of date. The Archbishop of Mainz has been persuaded so far to demean his own dignity as to accept a cardinal's hat, making him one of the Roman pontiff's monks' (891:27-33). He congratulated a Benedictine abbot for not spending his time in games of hazard or hunting, but 'encouraging the study of Holy Scripture, the spring from which all holiness of life must flow, in order to restore the ruined discipline of the religious life' (894:18-25).

Although so many people had been delighted to get his Latin New Testament, there were others who strongly disapproved of it, 'roundly declaring I can neither think nor write and that out of what I publish things can be sucked that will poison the faith'. He was amazed at the hostility with which 'friars and divines stone my New Testament' (876:13-16). For years he had to contend with detailed criticisms from Edward Lee, who was one day to become Archbishop of York. From less learned opponents he had to live with vicious attacks 'aroused by some avenging fury'. On the whole he felt that 'this serpent cannot be overcome by fighting back, and so I have said farewell to warfare and am taking shelter in the harbour of Christian gentleness, consoling myself in face of hostile critics with the opinions formed of me by men of good will' (952:26-29).

One of many who encouraged him was the Vicar-General of Constance. 'Separated we may be by so many mountains and the immense stretch of travel that lies between us, yet my eyes can always rest with pleasure on the products of your more than human genius. When I look into them, as I often do, I look upon their author in a truer sense than those who greet you face to face and grasp your hand in theirs. Countless people in Germany meditate upon the outcome of your nightly vigils. Countless people under your guidance have rubbed off the rust of traditional ignorance and are now making great strides towards bearing fruit. Need I mention myself? In years gone by I enjoyed your delightful society and you so caught hold of me and transformed me that you almost made me another person. I do not doubt that the New Testament newly enriched by you is a magnificent work. I look for its appearance more eagerly than ever mother did for a beloved son returning from foreign parts' (953:9-68).

It was in a letter sent to Erfurt while Erasmus was still convalescent in October 1518 that the name of Luther first appears in his surviving correspondence. 'I imagine his Theses satisfied everyone, except for a few of them on purgatory, which leading people are loth to lose because of its effect on their daily bread. I perceive that the absolute rule of a certain high-priest, as that See is now run, is the curse of Christianity. I fear the princes are in collusion with his Holiness, hoping for a share in the spoils. I cannot think what has come into Eck's head that he should take up the cudgels against Luther' (872:15-26). It was unusual for Erasmus to allude to Pope Leo in such terms, for he had dedicated to him the first edition of his New Testament and a few months later he told Cardinal Wolsey that 'if you test me at close quarters you will find in your Erasmus a whole-hearted servant of the Roman See, especially of our Holy Father Leo the Tenth' (967:218-219).

Luther first wrote to him on March 28, 1519, revealing what an important part Erasmus had played in his own development. 'Martin Luther to Erasmus of Rotterdam. Jesus. Greeting. Often though I converse with you and you with me, Erasmus my glory and my hope, we do not yet know one another. Is not this monstrous odd? And yet not odd at all, but a daily experience. For who is there in whose heart Erasmus does not occupy a central place, to whom Erasmus is not the teacher who holds him in thrall? I speak of those who love learning as it should be loved. While you are so highly approved by all men of good will, you are no less disapproved of by those who wish to secure the highest places and highest approval for themselves alone. But what a dolt am I to approach such a man as you with unwashed hands like this – no opening words of respect and reverence, as though you were a most familiar friend. Nor should I have allowed you alone to do all the talking as I sit here in my study. Having heard from my friend Wolfgang Capito that my name is known to you through the slight piece I wrote about indulgences, and learning very recently from the preface to the new edition of your *Handbook* that you have approved what I wrote, I feel bound to acknowledge that wonderful spirit of yours which has so much enriched me and all of us, although I know you are quite content with the gratitude and Christian love – secret and laid up in God's keeping – that burn within my heart when I think of you. Yet my sense of duty for all that you do for us in you books insists on being expressed in words, for if I keep silence I don't want anyone to think that this is due to jealousy. And so, dear Erasmus, kindest of men, if you see no objection, accept this younger brother of yours in Christ, who is at least much devoted to you and full of affection. The Lord Jesus preserve you, most worthy Erasmus, for ever and ever' (933:1-38, 53-54).

Encouraged by the warm reception given to his paraphrase of Romans, Erasmus spent several weeks drawing up paraphrases of Paul's Epistles to the Corinthians. 'There was a competition between the printer and myself, whether he could print off with his types every day more than I could write out with my pen. If only the liturgical matters Paul touches on here, and shows us as it were through a lattice, had been handed down by him more fully and more clearly! How concise is his mention of the eucharist, on which certain moderns hold forth at length. If only he had told us one thing at least: the persons, the time, the vestments, the rite, the wording customarily employed to consecrate the mystic bread and the cup that contains the Lord's most holy blood, from the unworthy handling of which, Paul tells us, spring frequently disease and death. And it is handled unworthily, not only by the man who approaches it when polluted by lust, but much more by him who is befouled with envy, hatred and malice, with scandal-mongering and a passion for revenge, which are diametrically opposed to Christian charity. He speaks rather more fully of the gift of tongues, of interpretation, of prophecy and other gifts, the place of which was later taken by church music, the reading of Scripture, and preaching. For the gifts of healing and apocalyptic vision have long since left us, since love grew cold, faith languished, and we learnt to depend on human resources rather than the help of heaven' (918:6-9, 916:62-84).

Alluding to Paul having delivered a man to Satan so that 'being shunned for a time by everyone, shame might bring him to repentance', Erasmus observed that this had been replaced by 'the terrifying thunderbolt of excommunication, in these days to my mind aimed indiscriminately and for the most frivolous reasons, never with more energy than when some sum of money is at risk' (915:85-96). And he denounced 'what are now commonly called indulgences' whereby 'remission of the torments of purgatory is openly hawked up and down, and not merely sold for money but forced upon those who do not want it, for reasons which in these days I will not mention' (916:133-140). Referring to the fifteenth chapter of 1 Corinthians, he was glad that during Paul's lifetime disputes were not about such things as indulgences, 'which we now drag by the scruff of the neck into the substance of the faith, but about the resurrection of the dead, which is the foundation and crown of our belief', although Erasmus knew of many prominent men, 'who live as if they had no belief whatever in a future life' (916:311-322).

He emphasised the problems Paul acknowledged in his second Epistle to the Corinthians: 'Although those who are born again in Christ ought to put off the old man with his deeds and affections, we see nevertheless that while the Gospel was still fresh under Paul's leadership, lust, avarice, strife, ambition, discord, and other pests of religion and morality had crept in among the people, while it had not been possible to root out certain vices left over from their former life. Let no one therefore be surprised if in our own day some men abound in iniquity, ready to turn the Gospel enterprise to their own profit, to preach themselves rather than God, the world in place of Christ, and the flesh in place of the Spirit, to gloss over heavenly teaching with the teachings of men. If only all those who have succeeded to the office of preaching the Gospel would follow Paul's example and preach Jesus Christ in sincerity and truth. If shepherds become wolves, what hope for the flock?' (916:335-360).

A priest, often employed on diplomatic missions by Henry VIII, wrote enthusiastically from London: 'I have read your paraphrase on the two Epistles to the Corinthians with the greatest care and wish to say that from this labour of yours I have gained so much that at long last I understand what Paul says and what he means. At last that divine Spirit in Paul has its full force and those divine precepts are turned to honey. Your paraphrase has made all so clear to me that I shall bid farewell to other commentaries by modern interpreters. Keep it up, my dear Erasmus, I do beg you, and explain the other Pauline Epistles in the same way. The reading of what I have seen was so enjoyable and so profitable as to make me wait eagerly for what is yet to come. It is a task fully worthy of your genius' (937:14-39).

In the summer of 1519 a young German priest, Justus Jonas, professor of canon law at Erfurt University, came to visit Erasmus with one of his colleagues. 'Through forests infested with brigands and cities infested with plague we have made our way to you, dear Erasmus. It was a tedious journey, but while we were still uncertain where you, the one special pearl of Christendom, were lying hid, we solemnly swore that we would seek you in farthest India or ultimate Thule. I have learned at home to know you by your books. You are the great privilege of this generation, given us by Christ himself' (977:1-14). When they at last got to Louvain, Erasmus was not there, but they eventually found him on the seashore near Antwerp. An earlier letter from Jonas had greatly impressed him – 'what power it had to move one and touch the heart in many ways' – so he was delighted by his unexpected appearance. 'Everything I saw in Jonas gave me particular satisfaction. I regard him as a chosen instrument for the enhancement of Christ's glory in the thick darkness of our time' (978:16-19). With the words of 1 Corinthians still fresh in his mind, he wrote to him one of his most memorable letters.

'Although Almighty God had it in his power to endue each individual man with every gift, yet he thought it more appropriate to distribute his gifts, one to this man and another to that, in such a way that men were obliged to help one another and that none should trust unduly in himself alone. God's gifts are distributed to different members of the same body. You must do what you can for the body where you can do it best. On this point I find some people lacking in wisdom, who before they are really acquainted with themselves plunge into some way of life in which they can be of no use to themselves or to others. This train of thought immediately entered my head as I conjured up an image of your mind from what you write and the manner of man you are. Although I suppose you know something of yourself, yet I thought I should tell you this: God did not design you for the law-courts, but he seems rather to have made you as a chosen instrument for the greater glory of Jesus, to kindle the souls of mortal men with zeal for him. You must devote all your powers to this life-giving activity, and that too in good time, while your frame can endure hard work and your mind retains its vigour. He who gave you a fervent heart, and a practised tongue to root out and to plant, will not fail you, especially if you keep no end in view except that Christ may gain. It may be splendid to move your hand in blessing over a multitude on its knees, it may be a great thing to administer the sacraments of the church, but unquestionably the noblest office and the most difficult of all is to offer the doctrine of salvation to the people and make their thoughts and their life worthy of Christ. You are too sensible to need to be told by me that it does more to implant the philosophy of Christ in men's minds if one presents it in as lively colours as one can: the face of virtue has a power of its own. It will add not a little force to what you say if your teaching is drawn principally from Holy Writ, if your life answers to your teaching, and if you proceed to your pulpit not from profane conversation but from concentrated prayer, that you may kindle the hearts of others with fire in your own heart' (967A:5-126).

When he received this letter Jonas was twenty-seven years old. Shortly afterwards he became rector of Erfurt University, introducing Greek and Hebrew into its curriculum. Then he moved to Wittenberg University where, as Luther's friend and colleague, he shared with him in bringing about the Reformation.

13

I Keep Myself Uncommitted

Reply to Luther; marriage; Cicero; Bohemia

1519: Louvain

'Dearest brother in Christ', were the first words in Erasmus' reply to Luther. 'Your letter gave me great pleasure: it displayed the brilliance of your mind and breathed the spirit of a Christian. No words of mine could describe the storm raised here in Louvain by your books. Even now it is impossible to root out from men's minds the most groundless suspicion that your work is written with assistance from me and that I am, as they call it, a standard-bearer of this new movement. They are under the impression that I contribute something of importance towards this outburst of zeal. Their weapons are clamour, audacity, misrepresentation and innuendo. I would never have believed theologians could be such maniacs. A great part of the university has been carried away by the contagion of this epidemic paranoia. I assured them that you were quite unknown to me, that I had not yet read your books and could therefore neither disprove nor approve anything. I did no good at all; they are so blinded. I would paint them in their true colours, as they deserve, did not Christ's teaching and Christ's example point in quite another direction. You have people in England who think well of what you write and they are in high place. As for me, I keep myself uncommitted, so far as I can. I think one gets further by courtesy and moderation than by clamour. That was how Christ brought the world under his sway. Things which are of such wide acceptance that they cannot be torn out of men's minds all at once should be met with close-reasoned forcible argument, rather than bare assertion. Some people's poisonous propaganda is better ignored than refuted. We must take pains to do and say nothing out of arrogance or faction, for I think the spirit of Christ would have it so. We must keep our minds above the corruption of anger or hatred, or of ambition; for it is this that lies in wait for us when our religious zeal is in full course. I am not instructing you to do this, only to do what you do always. May the Lord Jesus ever more richly endue you with his spirit every day, for his own glory and the good of mankind. Farewell from Louvain, May 30, 1519' (980:1-21, 36-59).

Erasmus revealed another aspect of his thinking in a letter written the same day to a close friend of Luther. 'In these parts the papal party is thus far in full cry, the whole pack being at last of one mind, to do mischief. The best men all support Luther's idea of liberty. I do not doubt that his wisdom will ensure the affair does not issue in discord and rupture. I believe our objective should be to implant Christ in the hearts of men, rather than to fight in the arena with men who wear the mask of Christians, from whom victory will never be won until the tyranny of the Roman See has been abolished' (983:8-16).

He took the risk of addressing one of the inquisitors who had bitterly criticised him for doubting that remarriage after divorce was unlawful. 'How you put venom in everything', Erasmus dared to say, 'how treacherously you distort that I have written, continually interpreting it as an attack on the church'. Very cautiously he tried to explain: 'I record my pity for people who are loosely held together by an unhappy marriage and yet would have no hope of abstaining from fornication if they were released from it. I want to secure their salvation by some means, nor have I any wish for this to happen without the consent of the church. I am no innovator. But it is possible that the spirit of Christ may not have revealed the whole truth to the church all at once. And while the church cannot make Christ's decrees of no effect, she can none the less interpret them as may best tend to the salvation of men, relaxing here and drawing tighter there, as time and circumstance may require. Christ wished that all his people might be perfect, no question of divorce arising among them, and the church has endeavoured to secure this full rigour from everyone. I am no supporter of divorce. But how can you be sure that the same church, in her zeal to find a way for the salvation even of weaker brethren, may not think that this is the place for some relaxation? The Gospel is not superseded; it is adapted by those to whom its application is entrusted, so as to secure the salvation of all men. My opinion is that we are misusing the interpretation of the gospel principles, with the result that the force of its teaching in our standards of behaviour is fading away. To give an example, Christ so wished his people to abstain from murder that he did not permit men to be angry. We interpret this as meaning angry without just cause. Likewise Christ so wished his people to abstain from perjury that he forbade an oath of any kind. This we interpret as meaning that we must not swear without just cause. In the same way he so much wished them to abstain from divorce that he forbade it altogether. What interpretation the church can put upon this, I do not decide. I wish she could interpret it so as to promote many men's salvation. I do not make any final proposals on this point. I leave the right of decision to the church and content myself with drawing attention to the point' (1006:180-259).

Looking back later on, and when writing to a friend, he revealed more of his thinking. 'I have always maintained that priests who are to be ordained in the future need not be forbidden to marry if they cannot remain continent, nor would I change my view if I were dealing with the Pope himself, not that I do not value continence more highly, but because I see almost none who remain continent. I have never advised a man to marry, but neither have I caused trouble for a man who wished to marry' (1477B:107-114).

By August 1519 Erasmus for once felt that he needed to get away from his study 'to restore and repair my strength of mind and body', so for some weeks he had a holiday visiting several towns in Flanders. 'Even so, I could not endure to be so wholly parted from my beloved library as not to carry round with me two or three books, among them a small volume of Cicero which attracted me because it would not add much weight to my luggage. From reading this I gained a double benefit. I refreshed the memory of my early intimacy with him in a way that gave me extraordinary pleasure. And then I so fired my whole self with a zeal for honour and virtue that for a long time I had felt nothing of the kind while reading some modern authors who are Christians, teach the mysteries of Christian philosophy with great subtlety and yet leave us quite cold.

I frankly confess that as I read Cicero I found myself thinking: is this a pagan writing for pagans? What purity, what sincerity, what truth in his rules for living, all in harmony with nature, nothing glossed over or half asleep. What a loveable picture of virtue he paints before our eyes! How many lessons he teaches and how like a saint – almost a deity! – on how we should do good to all men even without reward, on the maintenance of friendship, on the immortality of souls, on contempt for the things for whose sake the modern public – not merely ordinary Christians but divines and monks as well – will do anything. Meanwhile I was ashamed at the thought of our own behaviour: brought up on the Scriptures, encouraged by such examples and such rewards, we profess the gospel teaching and do not practise it. What a disgrace it is that a heart illuminated by the light of the Gospel should not see what was clearly seen by pagans with only nature's candle to show them the way, who suspected or fully believed that no part of a man survived the funeral pyre' (1013:27-77). He had already published Cicero's writings in 1501, but now he had an enlarged edition with his own notes published by Martens in Louvain and Froben in Basel. So he did indeed have a truly Erasmian holiday. The experience quickened his sense that such classical authors as Cicero, Seneca, and Plutarch had unconsciously been precursors of true Christianity.

On September 16, 1519 John Colet, the dean of St. Paul's, died in London. The news was intensely distressing to Erasmus. 'I feel only half a man, with myself alive and Colet dead. How that man had drunk in the philosophy of Christ, how greedily he had absorbed the spirit of St. Paul, and how the purity of his life echoed that heavenly doctrine.

He will never return to us. We shall go to join him. But what good does it do to weep and wail? I know that it is well with him. He is at peace; released from this wicked and miserable world, he enjoys face to face the presence of his master Christ, whom in life he loved so much. Let us rejoice with him. But for the general good I am bound to lament the loss of such an outstanding preacher of Christian truth' (1025:1, 1030:45-49, 1053:582-5). And he himself was deprived of 'the most reliable of my friends' at a time when he was at the centre of a fierce storm of hostility in Louvain, 'contrived by the machinations of Satan, who hates nothing more than the sight of Christians at peace and uses every means, including the pretext of religion, to break up the tranquillity of life and learned work' (1033:30-35).

Although two years had passed since Luther's theses had made him widely known, there was as yet no open breach between him and the Catholic Church. He was just a tiresome German theologian appealing to Scripture against the Pope, challenging long established customs and beliefs at the risk of his life. Erasmus' special problem was that he himself was blamed for this increasingly threatening situation north of the Alps. So he tried to explain himself to Archbishop Albert of Mainz. 'I have not yet found time to read Luther's books. I did my best to prevent the publication of some of them, for I was afraid they would give rise to disorders. I do not accuse Luther and I do not defend him. I am not answerable for him. If he has written well, none of the credit is due to me. If the reverse, there is nothing that can be laid at my door. One thing I do see: it is the best men who take the least offense at what he writes. If he is innocent, I should be sorry to see him overwhelmed by some villainous faction. If he is wrong, I would rather he were set right than destroyed' (1033:45-77).

He was convinced that the Archbishop ought to know of the venomous attacks on Luther which had become normal among theologians in Louvain University, how they ranted and railed against him, bent on his annihilation, 'thirsting for nothing but human blood, all agape for nothing so much as to seize him and destroy him'. In Erasmus' opinion, 'this is to play the butcher, not the theologian'. It was also a warning of what he could expect himself, if he were not careful. 'We must look clearly at the sources of this evil. The world is burdened with ordinances, opinions, and dogmas made by man, with the tyranny of the mendicant friars who, though they are servants of the Roman See, have risen to such influence and such numbers that the Pope himself finds them formidable. With growing effrontery they now begin to leave Christ out of it and preach nothing but their own impudent new dogmas, sapping the vigour of the gospel teaching. The centre of religion was tending to be ceremonial. It was these things that roused Luther to take the first bold step about indulgences. He made bold to speak, with some moderation, of the power of the Roman pontiff. He made bold to condemn the pronouncements of Thomas Aquinas, set almost above the Gospels. He made bold to discuss some doubtful points on the subject of confession, on which the monks set traps for men's consciences. All this was torment to religious minds, who in sermons heard very little about Christ but almost everything about the powers of the papacy and the opinions of modern authorities. It is their fault, I think, even if Luther was rather too intemperate. We have, I should suppose, a pious pope, but in such a stormy sea there is much of which he is unaware. It is no secret that there are people who seek to arouse his holy fervour against Luther. What hurts their feelings worst of all is that he does not attach much importance to Thomas Aquinas and that he thinks the man-made subtleties of academic disputation can be ignored. On the slightest pretext they all cry "Heresy, heresy". Anything they don't like or don't understand is heresy. To know Greek is heresy. To speak like an educated man is heresy. Anything they don't do themselves is heresy' (1033:131-267).

In November 1519 Erasmus wrote to a friend in Prague, formerly secretary to the King of Bohemia. 'I used to think I had some moderate experience of human affairs, having lived in different countries with various kinds of men, but I have found such monsters among Christians as I would never have believed had I not learnt the reality to my great misfortune. Perhaps it has pleased God that in this way I should atone for my misdoings, by which I offend against him frequently. I will forgive them, that he in turn may forgive me. It seems to me astonishing that nothing can be thought of so monstrous that it finds no followers. Some still follow the foolish doctrines of Epicurus and deny that our souls survive after death. What does a man believe who denies the immortality of the soul? Some regard Judas the betrayer as the saviour of the world and worship him as the supreme god. Others hold that private property is impious, spend their lives in idleness, live on alms, and reject as irreligious those who obtain by their own labours the wherewithal to maintain their wives and children. Some chant innumerable psalms all day long and do nothing else: this lunacy finds its adherents. Others maintain that those who strictly uphold the sanctity of marriage are more wicked than those who demand that wives be held in common. This makes it all the more important not to teach anything which does not square with the rule laid down by Christ. If avarice and ambition have power over us, if our lusts are too criminal, our hatreds too cruel, our envy too damaging, our malice too poisonous, to what end do we acknowledge Christ, who was made man in order to wean us away from such things? If anyone wishes to be indignant with me for saying this, let him be indignant with the apostle James, who says it all with emphasis in his Epistle' (1039:4-103).

Then Erasmus addressed himself to the situation in Bohemia where there were two other Christian movements apart from the Catholic Church. He could not agree that 'the Roman pontiff is Antichrist because there has now and then been an impious Pope, or that the Church of Rome is the great harlot because it sometimes has wicked cardinals or bishops'. Having said that, he proceeded to commend the papacy in terms very different to what he had been using before Luther came on the scene. 'What comes closer to the design of the hierarchy of heaven than a system of ordered ranks culminating in a single head? What could be more valuable as a defence against the divisions of the world? If some prince designs to seize despotic power, he will be kept in his place by the exhortations and prayers, the teaching and authority of the Holy See. If some bishop behaves like a tyrant, the common people will have somewhere to apply for help. Should someone arise who brings in the devil's doctrine, the Roman shepherd will be there to bring forth from the pure sources of gospel philosophy things worthy of Christ's steward and vicegerent. We should also remember that while he presides over mankind, he is but man himself and that if mutual concord is to last long he must be mild and give us our head in many ways, but we in our turn must obey him as the times demand, especially since the apostle teaches us that we must obey even wicked and wayward princes as far as we can without doing violence to our religion' (1039:106-124).

Had he forgotten what he said so recently about the tyranny of the Roman See (983:15)? Or had he now changed his opinion, hoping to regain acceptance after being blamed for what Luther was doing?

Hearing that one of the Bohemian groups 'received the Eucharist in both kinds', in wine as well as bread, unlike Catholics, he suggested 'their opinion on this question may well be true, and to say frankly what I think, I wonder very much why it was thought right to alter what was instituted by Christ himself'. Yet he admitted that if his advice had been asked, 'I should have told them to comply rather than stand out, as the greatest part of Christendom follows this custom'. This preference for 'the rule of concord' in contrast to what he knew to be strictly true was becoming crucial to him. He brought it up again over wearing vestments. 'Although it is not untrue that Christ and the apostles celebrated in everyday clothes, yet it is wrong to despise a custom instituted later by the Fathers. They are only ceremonies, but these ceremonies make the holy mysteries more acceptable to the people' (1039:125-140, 169-173).

Erasmus felt that many Bohemians could be reconciled to the Roman church 'if only such things were defined as are clearly laid down in Holy Writ, without which our salvation cannot stand. For this a few truths are enough and the multitude are more easily persuaded of their truth if they are few. The whole of the Christian philosophy lies in this, our understanding that all our hope is placed in God, who freely gives us all things through Jesus his Son, that we were redeemed by his death and engrafted through baptism into his body, that we might be dead to the desires of this world and live by his teaching and example, so that if adversity befall us we may bear it bravely in hope of the future reward, which beyond question awaits all good men at Christ's coming, and that we may ever advance from one virtue to another, claiming nothing for ourselves but ascribing any good we do to God. These are the things that must be implanted in the hearts of men' (1039:239-255).

This precise statement of what he meant by the philosophy of Christ was derived from Paul's magnificent summary of the gospel in chapters 2 and 3 of his Epistle to Titus, which Erasmus was paraphrasing just at that time. In contrast to these great truths he felt that 'to pursue abstruse questions touching the divine nature, the substance of Christ, or how the bread is made to change its character by the mystic words and how the same body can exist in so small a form and in different places – all this contributes very little to true religion and diverts men's minds from the only things that really matter' (1039:256-280).

14

Confusion and Danger

Many paraphrases; Melanchthon and Luther; escape

1519-1520: Louvain

In the winter of 1519-1520 Erasmus determined to complete his paraphrases of the Pauline Epistles. 'In these months, though the fields lie bare and barren everywhere, the good corn-land of literature never ceases to bear some kind of crop, nor is midwinter ever so bleak that the harvest-carts of learning cannot come home full' (1043:3-6). His paraphrases of Romans in 1517, of both Corinthian Epistles in January 1519 and of Galatians in May 1519 had been warmly welcomed. So now he turned to 1 Timothy, 2 Timothy, and Titus, together providing such 'a wonderfully vivid picture of a really Christian prelate', and also Philemon 'in order not to leave it out in the cold'. These were printed at the year's end, and by February 1520 Dirk Martens was publishing his paraphrases of Ephesians, Philippians, Colossians, and the Thessalonian Epistles, all five completed in one spell of work. 'In olden days the Christian philosophy was a matter of faith not of disputation', he said in the preface. 'Men's simple piety was satisfied with the oracles of Holy Scripture and unselfish love was a natural growth which had no need of complicated rules. Later on the management of theology was taken in hand by men nurtured in other fields of learning. Gradually philosophy came to be applied more and more, Platonic first and then Aristotelian, and questions began to be asked pertaining to morals or speculation about heavenly things. At first this seemed almost fundamental, but it developed by stages until many men, neglecting the study of the ancient tongues, of good literature and even of holy writ, grew old over questions meticulous, needless, and unreasonably minute. Theology began to be a form of skill, not wisdom; a show-piece, not a means toward true religion; and it was spoilt by ambition and avarice, flattery, strife, and superstition. Thus at length it came about that the pure image of Christ was almost overlaid by human disputations; the crystal springs of the old gospel teaching were choked with sawdust; and the undeviating rule of Holy Scripture, bent this way and that, became the slave of our appetites rather than of the glory of Christ' (1062:21-43).

By May he had moved on to the Epistles of Peter, 'under whose leadership the genuine philosophy of the gospel was first promoted' (1112:27), and the Epistle of Jude.

It was just as well that he was profitably occupied with these studies, for Luther's increasing prominence put him under exceptional pressure in Louvain. 'Gangs of conspirators hold forth against me at drinking parties and in taverns, in markets and shops, at the barbers' and in brothels, in classrooms, in university lectures, in sermons too, making me into an object of universal hatred' (1053:423-435). And he himself increased his troubles by a prolonged campaign of animosity against Edward Lee, the critic of his New Testament. 'This whole miserable business of Lee knocked me sideways' (1117:30). So much theological venom made it a sad period in his life, yet through it all he took refuge in 'the paradise of Holy Scripture, where we can pace slowly at our leisure, where we can cool our hot and weary hearts, where we can breathe a freer air and pluck the sweetest fruits' (1053:545-548).

Pirckheimer was concerned about him, having 'read this most tedious attack by Edward Lee' and then studied Erasmus' reply. 'Would you like to know what I think? I wish you had either kept silence or answered the man as he deserved, with no restraint at all, loosing off the whole armoury of your eloquence against his poisonous invective. I beg you, for the sake of your reputation and in the name of our mutual friendship, not to think in future that every noisy rascal deserves a reply. Remember who you are – too big a man to descend into such an arena with men like him, from which even as the victor you can win nothing but disgrace. Unless you do this, a mob of malignant scribblers must in the end overwhelm you. For these men never rest: they rave all the time against merit and scholarship and truth itself' (1095:11-46).

On June 15, 1520 Pope Leo issued his bull against Luther, beginning with the words, 'Arise, O Lord, and judge thy cause. A wild boar has invaded thy vineyard'. Forty-one of his errors were specified. His books were to be burned. He himself was given sixty days to submit. 'Anyone who presumes to infringe our excommunication and anathema will stand under the wrath of Almighty God.'

A few days later, knowing nothing of the bull, Erasmus wrote to Philip Melanchthon, professor of Greek at Wittenberg University alongside Luther. 'I am in favour of Luther as far as one can be, although people everywhere connect what he stands for with what I stand for. I greatly enjoyed his answer to the condemnation by his enemies in Louvain. His supporters – and they include almost all men of good will – would wish that some of what he has written were more courteously and moderately expressed, but it is too late to tell him so now. I can see that things are heading towards civil strife. I pray it may serve Christ's glory. As for that lot, I can see their machinations are diabolical, to put down Christ and set themselves up as tyrants in his name. Remember me to Dr Luther and to all your friends' (1113:15-40).

He admitted that in writing to Melanchthon he had the feeling he was writing to Luther as well. 'I pray that Christ Almighty may moderate Luther's pen and his mind in such a way that he may be the greatest benefit to the religion of the Gospel and bring into a better frame of mind those people who seek their own glory at the price of Christ's shame. In the ranks of Luther's opponents I see many who smack of his world rather than Christ. Yet there are mistakes on both sides. How I wish Luther would take a rest for some time from these controversies and treat simply the facts of the Gospel with no personal feeling mixed in. Perhaps we might see better results. As it is he burdens himself with unpopularity. The truth need not always be put forward and it makes a great difference how it is put forward' (1119:32-46). These words, written on July 6, 1520, with which he tried in vain to apply the brake to Luther's progress, indicate that his own long campaign for a better church was already being superseded by a faster and riskier reform, driven forwards by a daring man of action. 'Good literature should make its way into our universities not with the air of an enemy who will lay waste all before him, but as a guest who will grow gradually into union with his fellow-citizens. I have never liked disorder and, unless I am quite blind, a moderate policy is more effective than uncontrolled violence. Indeed, I think it is the duty of all good men to wish to benefit their fellows in such a way that they hurt very few, or none at all if that is possible. Theology, frigid and quarrelsome, had sunk to such a pitch of futility that it was essential to recall it to the fountain-head. Even so, I would rather see correction here than destruction, or at least toleration, until some better approach to theology is forthcoming. Luther has rendered a great service by pointing out so many abuses, but I wish he had done so in more civil language. He would have more supporters and more champions, and would reap for Christ a richer harvest. And yet it would be quite wrong, where he has said what wanted saying, to leave him without support, or in the future no one will dare to speak the truth. It is not for one in my position or with my endowments to pass judgment on his teaching. Hitherto, there is no doubt, he has done a service to the world at large' (1127:10-27).

On August 1, 1520 he wrote again to Luther. 'Greeting. I am not the right man, my dear Luther, to give you advice, but if you entirely reject all philosophy, you will have on your hands not only all universities but even your favourite Augustine, whom you follow so readily. Even granted that philosophy were to be entirely rejected, it will be unwise to take on so much at once. Hair by hair gets the tail off the mare. The King of England asked me what I thought of you. I replied that you were too good a scholar for a man with too little learning to be able to form an opinion about you. He expressed the wish that you had written some things with more prudence and moderation. That wish is shared, my dear Luther, by those who wish you well. It is a serious matter to challenge men who cannot be overthrown without a major upheaval. And I fear upheavals of that kind all the more, because they so often burst out in a different direction from what was intended. If a man lets in the sea, it is not in his power to control where it should go. If an upheaval is required by the state of things, I would rather someone other than myself took the responsibility. But I shall not oppose your policy, for fear that, if it is inspired by the spirit of Christ, I may be opposing Christ. You have had quite enough controversies with Eck and with everyone else. I wish you would write a treatise on some part of Holy Scripture and keep personal feelings out of it. It may be that in the mean time this turmoil will die down. Farewell, dearest brother in the Lord. To the Reverend Dr Martin Luther, the eminent theologian' (1127A:51-56, 64-77, 97-106).

It must again be remembered that as yet there was no new Christian community, only a very articulate German professor challenging the all-powerful Catholic system, including the papacy. The most probable outcome was that he would be burnt at the stake as John Hus had been a century earlier, in spite of receiving a safe-conduct to attend the Council of Constance.

But Luther had no intention of taking a rest or modifying his proclamation of the truth. On the contrary he poured out a torrent of pamphlets and books which greatly increased the tension. In August 1520 came his *Address to the German Nation*, in September *The Babylonian Captivity*, his radical critique of the sacraments, the mass and the priesthood, followed in October by *Against the Execrable Bull of Antichrist*, and in November *The*

Freedom of the Christian Man asserting the priesthood of all believers. Then on December 10, sixty days after receiving the bull, he burnt it publicly at the gate of Wittenberg – not at all Erasmus' way of doing things.

Bitter hostility to Luther, so far away, was expressed at Louvain in daily antagonism to Erasmus close at hand. 'Few men, perhaps, feel the pain of all this uproar over Luther as much as I do' (1144:5). He was extremely busy, resisting Edward Lee's attacks on his New Testament, editing the voluminous writings of Augustine, composing his paraphrase of the Epistle to the Hebrews and the Epistle of James, as well as coping with his extensive correspondence. 'When your letter reached me I hardly had time to read it', he told a stranger. 'And later, when I had leisure, it lay hidden among bundles of letters so effectually that after careful search it could not be found for some months. At length it turned up unlooked-for, of its own accord. I put it on one side to await my first free moment, and it was again lost, I cannot tell how' (1147:5-11).

To try to clear his name he wrote to Pope Leo on September 13, 1520. 'Luther I do not know, nor have I ever read his books, except maybe for a mere ten or twelve pages, and those in snatches. From the samples I tasted he seemed to me admirably equipped as an expositor of Scripture. I therefore supported the good qualities in him and not the bad. I was almost the first person to detect the risk that the affair might issue in public strife, a thing I have always detested, so I actually used threats to dissuade Froben from printing any of his works. I could not refute him unless I had first read him carefully two or three times and for that I had no leisure' (1143:14-25, 57-58).

Meanwhile Luther's books were burnt in various cities

and in Louvain itself in October. A Carmelite friar preaching in St. Peter's Church 'began to direct his remarks against me, for by chance I had just entered, saying among many other things that I was a keen supporter of Luther and had tried to defend him with all my might'. The following Sunday he said much the same, adding that 'these men will come to the stake one day unless they desist' (1153:20-24, 47, 100-103).

Surrounded with such antagonism, 'I am filled with forebodings. The conspiracy against Luther is strong everywhere. A bull is in print, a terrific affair. I am having nothing to do with this miserable business. It grieves me to see the doctrine of the Gospel so lost to sight and ourselves exposed to compulsion' (1141:10-40). 'A desperate tragedy is now being enacted and what will happen in the last act is uncertain. They are as indignant with me as they are with Luther himself, supposing me to be the only obstacle which prevents his complete destruction. I see clearly enough that the business is too big for a small man like me. I am daily stoned with a hail of abuse in sermons' (1155:7-12, 1157:7-11, 1176:15-17).

His friends became extremely anxious about his unpopularity in Louvain: 'They have burnt Luther's books. Do you think you can stay in peace where you are, as though the men who have condemned Luther would spare you? Escape, dear Erasmus, escape while you can. These fellows are clamouring openly that it was you who began it all, that you first kindled men's minds with zeal for liberty, that you are the fountain-head of the Pope's present troubles. You have treated the Pope gently all these years, sung his praises and buttered him up, and what have you got from it? Your friends in Basel are longing to see you.

What holds you from moving to join them as soon as you can? Nowhere do men enjoy more liberty, and at the moment they are wonderfully excited by what Luther writes. Give some weight to the prayers of us all. Have the sense to avoid an obvious risk. Don't forget that poison works in secret' (1161:7-10, 107-122).

It was regrettable that at such a critical time, 'when things have moved so far towards the edge of chaos' (1155:33), he was surrounded not by the warm friends working in Froben's press but by the hatred of critics and opponents. His mind vacillated unhappily, at times cautiously praising Luther, yet often critical of his outspokenness, and uncharacteristically refusing to study him properly, though he longed to see 'a means to end this sad business without a worldwide conflagration' (1156:11). On December 6 he wrote freely to the papal legate in England. 'Fanatics misuse the pulpit for their nefarious purposes. For the state of public morals the purity of the pulpit is more important than the sacred liturgy. He who handles the liturgy unworthily puts no man in jeopardy but himself. But he who misuses the pulpit defrauds the hearers, infects them with his own poison, and robs the sacred office of preaching of its authority. I was the first person to condemn Luther's books, at least to the extent that they seemed to envisage public disturbance, which I have always abhorred. I was the first to put obstacles in the way of them being published. I am almost the only man who has not read his books, yet from what I have dipped into rather than read I thought he had the natural endowment and the necessary zeal to blow the spark of gospel teaching into flame. The world, as though weary of teaching which lays so much emphasis on petty human inventions and rules, seemed to me to thirst for the pure living water drawn from the evangelists and apostles. In these terms I thought well of Luther, and yet I saw in him enough to cause me anxiety and suspicion. So I warned him of things I thought he should avoid. Had he taken my advice I do not doubt that he would find Pope Leo among the chief supporters of his enterprise, for I believe he values nothing so much as the glory of Christ, whose vicegerent he is. I warned Luther not to attack the Roman pontiff or condemn the monastic orders out of hand. I counselled him to examine his own heart to ensure he was not tainted with arrogance, anger, hatred or vainglory. I supported Luther in that I would rather see him set right than destroyed, cured than snuffed out. Pray be perfectly convinced that your friend Erasmus always was and always will be a zealous supporter of the see of Rome. I shall count any of its enemies my personal enemy. I will never be a leader in error. Let others court martyrdom; it is an honour of which I find myself unworthy' (1167).

This long letter, confusing and inconsistent, well reflects Erasmus' distress and unhappiness as 1520 drew to its close.

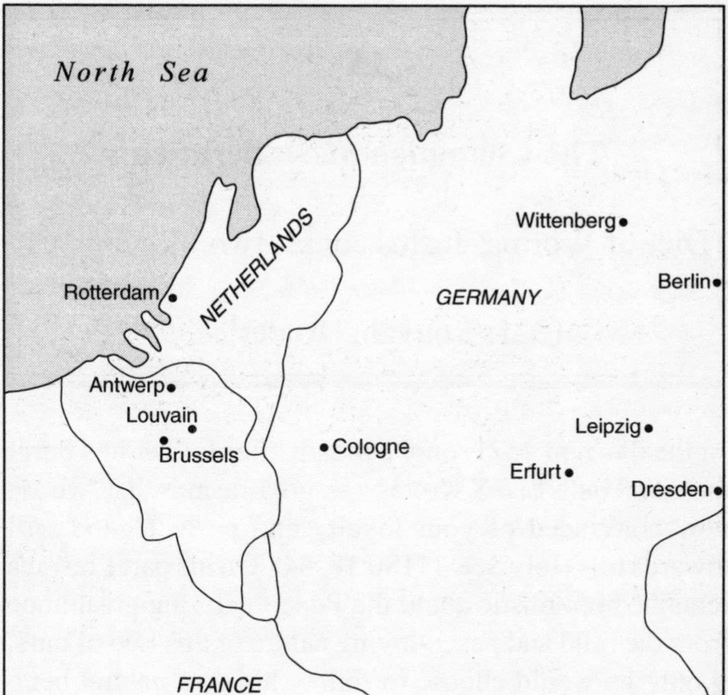

The Netherlands & Germany

15

The Champion of Moderation

Diet of Worms; Justus Jonas; two biographies

1521: Louvain, Anderlecht

At the dawn of 1521, only a month after Luther had burnt the papul bull, Leo X wrote to assure Erasmus that 'we are now convinced of your loyalty and perfect good will towards this Holy See' (1180:18, 34). On his part Erasmus remained optimistic about the Pope, 'deriving great hope from the mild and peace-loving nature of this Leo of ours, if only he would choose to follow his own natural bent, instead of favouring the prejudices of certain people who think more of their own personal advantage than of the interests of the world at large. The greatest part of all this tragic business of Luther has arisen from the inordinate greed of certain theologians, mainly Dominicans and Carmelites. It is clearly unfair to blame the Pope for everything that happens in Rome. Much is done without his knowledge, much that he dislikes, and against opposition from him. If Peter himself were to preside, he would be compelled, I suspect, to connive at some things which in his heart of hearts he could not possibly approve' (1183:22-26, 86-104).

But his main concern was 'this whirlwind of Luther'

raging around him. 'I have never approved the savagery of those who, before they have read Luther's books, declaim against him in public, using words like donkey and blockhead and heretic and Antichrist and universal pest. This is the sort of noisy rascals who defend the majesty of the papacy. The sole result of their uproar is to make more people buy Luther's books. A conspiracy of men has been formed to couple my name with his in their harangues, in order to overwhelm both of us. They regard me as an enemy because on occasion I have criticised Thomas Aquinas and because I have pointed out that true piety lies not in ceremonies but in a state of mind and heart, as well as urging young men not to be inveigled into the bonds of monastic life before they have learned to know themselves' (1183:118-150).

As February went on and Lent began, he deplored his plight. 'I am daily pelted with showers of abuse by the Dominicans even in their public sermons. Stephen was stoned once and his troubles were at an end, and he was attacked with nothing but stones. I am pelted often with lies dipped in deadly poison. In this wretched climate, with toilsome research, all the inconvenience of these noisy wretches, and fish-eating days, it is hardly possible to keep well' (1185:10-16, 1184:36-38). Meanwhile a Carmelite preaching before the King of France declared that the coming of Antichrist was imminent, his precursors being Jacques Lefèvre in Paris, Reuchlin in Germany, and Erasmus in Louvain (1192:29-33).

In his letters of March 1521 Erasmus admitted that Luther had by this time won substantial international support. 'The common people, and most educated people too, are attracted to him. No one would believe how much he has made his way into the minds of many nationalities and how deeply he has taken root in books which are circulating in all directions and in every language' (1192:70-73, 1192A:5-7).

Shortly before Luther travelled from Wittenberg to appear before the Diet of Worms in April, Erasmus summarised his own position. 'Those who appear to support Luther have done all they possibly can to lure me into his camp. His persecutors have tried to drive me into it, raving against me more offensively than they do against Luther himself. None of their tricks have succeeded. Christ I recognise, Luther I know not. The church of Rome I recognise and from that church death shall not tear me asunder. Subversion I have always loathed. Would that Luther and the Germans were all of that opinion! I perceive that in most regions this side of the Alps there are many who support Luther from a kind of destiny. No one does Luther more harm than himself with this stream of new and progressively more offensive pamphlets. Then the men who have no ideas except to eat Luther alive, bawl away in public with such ignorance and folly that they secure a welcome for him and damage the Pope's cause. I urge that in avoiding the Scylla of Luther we should not fall headlong into the Charybdis of this opposing faction, waiting to engulf the entire liberty of the people of Christ and extinguish the last spark of gospel teaching, this stupid sort of men who up to now by tricks and treachery have held despotic rule over Christ's flock, whose greed, pride, lust, and avarice nothing can satisfy. Avoid Luther as I may, I cannot all the same approve of men like this. I have no mind to differ by one hair's breadth from those who agree with the Catholic Church. I know that one should endure anything rather then upset the general state of the world and make it worse. I know that sometimes it is a good man's duty to conceal the truth and not to publish it complete. I know no faith but that of the Catholic Church. Such is the whole picture of my mind' (1195:29-46, 99-100, 109-124, 137-141, 1191:44-48).

Within a month Luther, speaking not before the Pope but in the presence of the Emperor Charles V at the Diet of Worms, gave a more lucid picture of his mind, taken captive by the Scriptures, the Word of God. 'Here I stand. I cannot do otherwise'. By the Edict of Worms, 'this devil in the habit of a monk, who lives the life of a beast, does more harm to the civil than to the ecclesiastical power, and recognises only the authority of Scripture interpreted in his own sense', was declared a convicted heretic. 'When three weeks is up, no one is to harbour him. His followers also are to be condemned. His books are to be eradicated from the memory of man.' Commanded by the Emperor to leave Worms, he set off for Wittenberg – and disappeared. Many people presumed he had been killed. But a friendly ambush had been arranged. On May 4 he was intercepted and whisked away to the safety of the mountaintop Wartburg Castle.

It seems a pity that Erasmus was not at Worms to meet and hear Luther. 'If I failed to attend the Diet, to which I had indeed been invited, the reason was partly that I did not wish to become involved with the Luther business, partly because my health was too uncertain to risk the journey and I could easily guess that in such a gathering there would certainly be plague' (1342:55-61, 1192A:22). Before he knew what had happened, Erasmus wrote another remarkable letter to young Justus Jonas, who had travelled to Worms with Luther and steadfastly supported him there. 'I doubt whether the princes of the church have ever displayed such a passionate and unconcealed appetite for the good things of this world as we see today. The breakdown was no less in the study of Holy Scripture than in morality. This was the reason why to start with Luther had such a favourable reception everywhere as has fallen to the lot of no other mortal, I suppose, for many centuries. People thought a man had arisen, unspotted by this world's desires, who would be able to apply some remedy to these great evils. Nor did I myself entirely despair of this. But once he had written with such freedom of invective against the Roman pontiff, the universities, philosophy and the mendicant orders, challenging so many people, I was full of fear that the thing might end in uproar and split the world in two. Seeing that truth of itself has a bitter taste for most people and that it is of itself a subversive thing to uproot what has long been commonly accepted, it would have been wiser to soften a naturally painful subject by handling it courteously' (1202:22-55).

He strongly denied that the situation was too grave to be 'healed by gentler remedies'. His long years of detailed study of the New Testament in Greek and Latin enabled him to set before Jonas an astonishing array of texts displaying Christ's example of courtesy and meekness, Paul's example of gentleness and Peter's example of mildness, though he failed to balance this by enumerating many occasions when Christ horrified and infuriated his hearers, while the apostles were stoned, beaten, imprisoned, and killed by religious people they had confronted. But Erasmus, forgetting, it might seem, how outspoken and critical he had been himself, had become the champion of moderation, of 'moderate measures' conveyed 'in a more moderate tone', characteristic of 'the modesty of a true Christian'. So 'above everything we must avoid discord: what is our religion if not peace in the Holy Spirit?' Time and again he advocated 'gentleness in teaching, gentleness in winning over those who are stubborn and hard to please' (1202:5-11, 73-124, 152).

And he continually maintained that 'sometimes it is right for truth to remain unspoken', pointing out that on the day of Pentecost Peter emphasised the prophecy of Joel, knowing it would carry weight with the Jews, but 'he did not yet declare that Christ is both God and man, reserving this until its proper time'. Luther, on the other hand, 'with a sort of immoderate energy, poured everything out at once, giving even cobblers a share in mysteries normally handled by scholars, whereas Christ said one thing to the somewhat thick-witted multitudes and another to his disciples. Luther might have done wonders for Christ's flock by teaching the philosophy of the Gospel, had he refrained from things that could not fail to end in strife' (1202:146, 66-94, 292-293).

Remembering his delight at Jonas' visit two years earlier, Erasmus wound up his letter with some exceptionally revealing admissions. 'My own work has lost a great part of the good effect I hoped for, thanks to Luther. If it were lawful to hate any man in return for wrongs suffered personally, no one has suffered more from Luther's party than myself. Although, to be quite frank, had I known that a generation such as this would appear, I should either not have written at all some things that I have written, or should have written them differently' (1202:295-299, 264-267).

In spite of being eclipsed by Luther, Erasmus was

incapable of idleness. His immediate task was a new edition of Augustine's works. 'My health gets more feeble every day, though my mind is as good as ever', he told the Archbishop of Canterbury. 'I should like to be granted length of days to rouse the minds of men still further to the genuine philosophy of Christ' (1205:25, 55-57). In May 1521 he felt so unwell that 'I set my mass of papers in order' and took them to the village of Anderlecht outside Brussels. 'This charming place and my host's kindness made a new man of me.' He stayed for five months at Anderlecht, engrossed in another revision of his Latin New Testament. Inevitably he took his troubles with him. 'Luther has cast an apple of discord into the world' (1228:30) and he feared worldwide disorders, 'though much of his teaching and many of his denunciations are admirable' (1218:33-35). Admitting that Christ cast merchants out of the temple, 'he never gave such instructions to his followers'. He felt it was lawful to keep silence about the truth if there was no hope of doing any good. 'Christ kept silence before Herod. An honourable silence is better than an ill-starred attempt at reform' (1219:111, 1217:109). In spite of all he had written himself and his unwise antagonism to Lefèvre and to Edward Lee, confronted with Luther's increasing success he maintained, 'I am always on the side of concord: my hatred of controversy is such that I dislike even truth that is subversive' (1225:322, 182).

From 'my county retreat at Anderlecht' he wrote a seven hundred line letter to Justus Jonas, who had asked him for an account of John Colet's life. Admiring Jonas and wanting to draw him away from Luther, Erasmus replied with a marvellous description not only of Colet but also of Jean Vitrier, a Franciscan monk, who 'in the ignorance of youth' had 'slipped into a way of life which by no means appealed to him. He used to say in my hearing that it was a life for idiots rather than religious men, to sleep and wake and sleep again, to speak and to be silent, to go and to return, to eat and to stop eating, all at the sound of a bell, and in a word to be governed in everything by human regulations rather than the law of Christ. Men with heaven-sent gifts, born for better things, were buried by ceremonies and petty man-made constitutions. Yet Vitrier never suggested to anyone that he should change his way of life, for he was ready to endure everything rather than be a cause of stumbling to any mortal man. Nothing was so unfair that he would not endure it with the greatest readiness in his desire for peace. The Holy Scriptures, and especially the Pauline Epistles, he had got by heart. Had you started him off anywhere, he would promptly have finished the whole Epistle without a slip. He did not divide his sermons under heads as the common run of preachers do, which is often the source of tedious subdivisions, nor make a parade of citing various authorities. He had a passion for bringing men into the true philosophy of Christ. His whole life was a sermon in itself. He was a jewel of a man, unknown to the world but famous in the kingdom of Christ' (1211:16-272).

Then Erasmus described Colet in even greater detail, his wealthy father, his mother – 'a woman of the highest character who bore her husband eleven sons and eleven daughters, Colet being the eldest of them all' – his wide studies, 'a pilgrimage through literature of every kind', his training in France and Italy, his lectures on Paul's Epistles in Oxford, 'till he was recalled to London by the favour of King Henry VII and made dean of St. Paul's'. He stressed

Colet's disciplined life. 'He was impatient of everything slovenly. His household gear, his clothes, his books, all must be neat. On his father's death he inherited an immense sum of money. For fear it would have a bad effect on him, he used it to build a school and a house for two masters, whose ample salaries enabled them to teach without demanding fees. His simple piety was only to a very small degree the result of his natural disposition. He was strongly disposed towards female society, self-indulgence and sleep, unusually inclined to joking, and not entirely immune to the love of money. Against these temptations he fought so successfully with the help of philosophy and sacred study and watching, fasting and prayer, that he passed his whole life unspotted by the defilements of this world. Sex, sleep, and luxury he put to flight by habitual abstention from supper, unwearying study and religious conversation. He had himself always under suspicion. I never met a more fertile mind, but he preferred to restrict himself to such topics as prepare us for immortality in the life to come. He used to say that he never found more uncorrupted characters than among married couples, for their natural affection, the care of their children, and the business of a household seemed to fence them in, so that they could not lapse indiscriminately into sin' (1211:273-605).

Reviewing what he had said about both men, Erasmus came to a surprising conclusion. 'It was a great thing that Colet in his station in life followed the call of Christ so steadfastly, yet Vitrier's achievement is more remarkable, for he demonstrated so much of the spirit of the Gospel in that sort of life, like a fish that lives in stagnant water' (1211:678-684). In fact Erasmus had begun to sense that it was Vitrier's example he himself would follow, enduring everything he knew to be wrong in his overriding desire for peace.

'The outstanding thing about Colet', he told a friend in Oxford, 'was the way he drew the genuine philosophy of Christ from the pure well-head of the Gospels. But to follow his example and entirely deny yourself dinner is a thing I do not approve, nor did I approve it in him. If you feel the need to bridle your bodily appetites, this would be better achieved by a moderate use of food and drink than by severe and continuous fasting. If you add to this self-discipline the vigorous and uninterrupted study of the Scriptures, there will be no need to torment yourself by fasting, which may perhaps keep the luxuriance of youth in check, but at the price of bequeathing an enfeebled constitution to your old age, and may restrain the fires of the body only to enfeeble the powers of the mind' (1229:12-28).

Even at Anderlecht he was still acutely conscious of the danger he was in. 'Such terror had seized everyone in Antwerp who had ever spared Luther a thought that scarcely anyone felt himself safe' (1318:16-17). He became convinced that 'unless Pope Leo himself keeps me safe to do him service, I do not see how I can be preserved, such is the determination with which certain individuals campaign against me; they even threaten dagger and poison; anyone can see what they would do, if they dared' (1236:144-150). But happily it became essential for him 'to assist at the birth of the New Testament for the third time' in Basel. On October 28,1521 he left Louvain and never again returned to the north.

16

You Belong to the Ages

Gospel paraphrases; Adrian; *Colloquies*; Zwingli

1521-1522: Basel, Constance

Many people were delighted to hear that Erasmus had arrived back in 'the noble German city of Basel' on November 15, 1521. 'Your return to us, my learned friend, is a matter of rejoicing in Germany and in all Christendom. We have waited for you as for a sun to dispel the darkness of our night, for you are the prime author of the revival of theology in our own time. You led us upstream to the crystal springs of the original Scriptures. It is a wonderful sight to see classical and sacred studies so interconnected that they can be pursued together without conflict. All this we owe to your efforts, your sleepless nights of scholarly activity. You have left no stone unturned to secure that the schools of theology should at long last recognise the divine philosophy of the cross. Rejoice, Erasmus, in your victory. It begins to be recognised, not among the learned only but by laymen too, that Scripture is the property of every Christian. I have no doubt at all that to breathe new life into theology is what you were born to do' (1235:1-31).

Although the journey south had not been quite so

devastating as the journey north in 1518, yet 'I had another attack of illness which put me in peril of my life. Nevertheless, half dead as I was, I finished a paraphrase of Matthew's Gospel. Even if one died in such a task, death would be holy. It is a joy to me to see the doctrine of the Gospels flourishing again. If only I could be successful in this enterprise to promote Christ's cause, as I have been in the apostolic epistles, which are thumbed everywhere' (1248:1-50). Originally he had not thought it possible to paraphrase a Gospel. 'There are some passages which, in my opinion, are quite inexplicable, such as the phrase about the sin against the Holy Spirit which can never be forgiven, and the last day which only the Father knows but is unknown even to the Son. In a commentary one can report the differing views of scholars or even confess that one does not understand a passage, but the author of a paraphrase is not allowed the same freedom' (1255:59-65). However, he yielded to persistent pressure from Cardinal Schiner in Switzerland, an enthusiast for his earlier paraphrases, 'urging me over and over again to leave no portion of this task to others' (1171: 52).

Only two weeks after his return to Basel, Pope Leo X died at midnight on December 1, aged only forty-five. Over New Year forty cardinals conferred together and arrived at a surprising decision. On January 9, 1522 they elected as the next pope Cardinal Adrian of Utrecht, aged sixty-two, who was a bishop in Spain and had not been consulted. Adrian was formerly dean of Louvain cathedral as well as professor of philosophy and theology at the University. Erasmus had once been among his students, so was to some extent acquainted with him and very pleased to hear such unexpected news. He wrote to congratulate him, suggesting that 'your advancing years will permit you to pursue no other goal except Christ's glory' (1304:376).

Apart from his sustained involvement in the theological problems of the church, Erasmus was achieving phenomenal success at quite a different level. In March 1522 Froben published an enlarged edition of his *Colloquies*, which had become immensely popular. 'I began it in Paris more than twenty years ago, when I had a mind to gossip after supper at the fireside and take my slippered ease' (909:11-13). The book had grown to be a succession of brief dialogues, comedies, and dramas depicting the struggles of women as well as men on a wide range of contemporary cultural, moral, and religious issues. Had Erasmus written nothing else, the *Colloquies* alone would have made him famous.

With Luther still hidden in the Wartburg and the new Pope out of sight in Spain, Erasmus was getting letters from Juan Luis Vives, the brilliant young Spanish scholar teaching at Louvain University. In the new edition of the works of Augustine, towards which Erasmus was working, he had deputed to Vives *The City of God*, Augustine's longest and greatest book. Vives was distressed to hear such 'wicked falsehoods and ceaseless propaganda' against Erasmus in Louvain. 'Your purpose is Christian, as it always was, and without doubt Christ has prepared for you a great reward, seeing what poor thanks you get from men who will not enjoy the perennial youth which is so entirely yours, the youth that comes from the classics and from Christ. You have done nothing wrong. You have played out the greater portion of your part in the drama of this life. In what remains, devote yourself to earning the approval not of the men you can see but of your conscience and of Christ, for whom you have endured so many labours. If you give any weight to the applause of the audience, let it be posterity rather than the present. When envy and all the other emotions are done away, posterity will contemplate in you the pure and true Erasmus and will give you the glory you deserve all the more generously in so far as the men of your own generation have been so unfair to you. This is what happened to Socrates. I beg you urgently not to distress yourself. You belong now to the ages. You can infer from the judgment of not a few men of good will what will be said of you among peoples yet unborn. If you consider this, you will reckon all the days of your life henceforward as pure gain, and you will live in peace and happiness. You will be, as it were, above the power of fate, my beloved teacher' (1256:17-101, 1271:105-125, 1306:77).

It was not easy for Erasmus to maintain such happiness. 'To both sides I am a heretic' (1268:31). 'Many Lutherans tear me to pieces as a Pelagian, thinking it wrong that I should attribute anything, however slight, to free will' (1259:13,14 and 1268:92-93). Yet he knew that the menace from the other side was much more dangerous. Many of his opponents, acting in the Pope's name, were 'busy tightening every noose of that ancient tyranny' (1268:11-13). He often found relief confiding in Pirckheimer. 'Personally, I do not find a faith extorted under compulsion of much value. Great is the authority of a papal bull, still greater that of the imperial decree in the Edict of Worms. Such things will perhaps keep men's tongues silent for a time. Whether they can convert men's minds, I do not know. Things have come to such a pass, so many abuses have crept in little by little, that something absolutely must be done to succour the liberty of all Christian people' (1268:24-35). At times he felt optimistic that the authority of the Emperor and 'the scholarly wisdom of our new Pope' would be able to cure 'this tragedy of the new gospel' by rooting out 'the intolerable greed and tyranny of the Roman curia' which lay behind it (1273:40-49).

It was a time of tremendous intellectual tension, as the experience of Oecolampadius suggested. After helping Erasmus with his New Testament, he got his doctorate in theology and became cathedral preacher in Augsburg. But the rise of Luther so perplexed him that he withdrew to a monastery, only to emerge in January 1522 in such strong support of 'the new gospel' that he was denounced in Rome as worse than Luther. Erasmus was correct in stating that 'Luther's way of thinking is not yet so extinct in men's bosoms as I myself would wish, for in this country there are more than a hundred thousand who hate the Roman See and to a great extent approve of him' (1299:31-34), while on the papal side many others were reading a publication entitled 'The Blasphemies and Impieties of Erasmus of Rotterdam', which set out to prove he was 'the standard-bearer and prime mover of Luther's party' (1290:1-5). Yet at the same time he deplored the fact that 'I have lost the friendship of innumerable scholars in Germany, because I made it clear that I do not think as Luther does. Those who used to describe me as the champion of sound learning and the prince of true theology, now find me less worth than seaweed' (1300:52-53 and 1341A:645-647).

On top of all this, his health had been deplorable ever since he returned to Basel. 'I have suffered repeated attacks of an illness which has now become so habitual that I fear it may never leave me. It is the most serious thing one can have, stone in the kidneys. It shows me less mercy every day. There is no end to it and no time off. One birth follows close on another, and several are in gestation all the time. The process of giving birth often puts me in grave peril of my life' (1283:8-10 and 1302:35-50). Moreover 'my personal sufferings are increased by the disastrous times we live in, the whole world plunged into savage wars by disputes between the Germans and the French. What a calamity for Christendom' (1283:11-13).

It must have been a great encouragement to him to hear from a Catholic bishop living far east of Prague. 'I cannot fail to admit, dear Erasmus, that I treasure the open-hearted letters you wrote me recently as highly as the most valuable gift I ever received. Could anything more precious come my way than for Erasmus, the great man of our time, the unchallenged leader in every branch of learning in both tongues, to admit me to be his friend when he has not yet met me? It is a long time since I first felt awe, respect, and admiration for you as a kind of divine being sent down to us from heaven. In all my travels I have you always as a companion at my elbow, for your most scholarly and pious writings make me not only a better scholar but a better man. And now that mutual affection has been added to all this, as I hope for salvation by the pleasure of our great Saviour, I know no words to express how much I rejoice to see you famous' (1272:1-29).

It was during this year that Zwingli wrote several times to Erasmus 'proposing that I should accept citizenship of Zürich, which surprised me very much' (1342:585-589). 'I am most grateful', he replied, 'to you and your city for your kindly thought. My own wish is to be a citizen of the world, a fellow-citizen to all men, a pilgrim. If only I might have the happiness of being enrolled in the city of heaven, for it is thither I make my way under constant attacks of illness. Nor do I see why I should want what you offer me. We shall soon see which way Christendom is turning. Our new pope is a theologian. For my part, as far as the world we live in allows, I shall not be wanting in Christ's service as long as I live. Fight on, dear Zwingli, not only with courage but with prudence too. Don't forget the modesty demanded by the gospel. Consult scholarly friends before you issue anything to the public. I fear that defence of yours, which I read, may land you in great peril and even do harm to the church. There was much in it on which I wanted to see you put right. I do not doubt that with your sound sense you will take this in good part, for I write with the warmest affection for you and late at night. Christ will grant that you fight with success' (1314:1-20, 1315:1-11).

Zwingli was indeed having great success as the leader of the Reformation in Switzerland. Conscious of his profound debt to Erasmus, he would have been glad to have his help rather than see him turn in the opposite direction.

Like everyone else, Erasmus was wondering about the attitude of his fellow-countryman, the new Pope. 'What he was like some time ago, I well know. What he will be like in such exalted office, I know not. Of one thing I am certain: he is entirely a scholastic theologian and not wholly well disposed to classical studies. But I have not forgotten his friendliness and loyal spirit. I get many letters from other people inviting me to Rome. Cardinal Schiner has offered me an annual salary as well as the expense of the journey, but I am terrified by the Alps and the Appennines, to which I doubt it would be safe to entrust a frail body like mine' (1311:15-26).

Adrian VI was a remarkable man. By his godliness, discipline, learning and devotion to duty he had risen from poverty to be a bishop, a cardinal, ruler of Spain on behalf of the Emperor, and now, to his astonishment and dismay, the Pope. A humble and unselfish person, horrified by the evils plaguing the Church, but Inquisitor-General in Spain and inflexibly opposed to Luther, he dreaded the burden thrust upon him, yet he felt it was his duty to God to take it up. Travelling in a flotilla of fifty ships for fear of Turkish pirates, he did not reach Rome till August 27, 1522, nearly eight months after his election. He had never been there before. Crowned four days later, he embarked immediately on radical reforms, sacking hundreds of people employed by his predecessor, living very simply with just three Dutch servants, reading mass every day, rising at dawn, working diligently in his study, totally opposed to immorality, as well as to the buying and selling of positions in the Church. Not accustomed to a Pope who was neither wealthy nor worldly nor wicked, a great many Romans were dismayed. Remembering that 'some men sat on the papal throne who sought not the things that are Jesus Christ's but, like that Demas condemned by the apostle Paul, were lovers of this world', Erasmus was hopeful. 'I wait to see which way the new pope will invite us to follow' (1313:32-34, 113).

In September, 'many people assuring me that it might be to my advantage if I presented myself before the new pope', Erasmus changed his mind and decided to head for Rome. He began by going to Constance, where he stayed for three weeks with Johann von Botzheim, whose home was a centre for artists and scholars. Apart from the fact that he was ill the whole time, it was a delightful experience. He could hardly eat anything and was only able to meet a few of the many who wanted to greet him. 'Presents arrived from all directions and for several days the town band played near by', so in spite of his weakness the visit turned into a kind of holiday and he even had time to revel in the surrounding scenery. 'Constance is dominated by a wonderful lake and by forest-clad hills in all directions. As though wearied by its passage through the Alps, the Rhine seems to have found a resting-place in which to recuperate. At Constance it gathers again into its proper channel, glides past the city, makes a smaller lake and then, full of whirlpools and cataracts, flows on to Schaffhausen, where it hurls itself over the falls with a great roar.' An Italian bishop, who was also bound for Rome, suggested they travel together. 'I was much attracted, for Trento was not more than six days distant from Constance. The two of us sat down and talked about all sorts of things. He was a man of great wisdom and long experience. The Alpine meadows smiled upon us, but my friends were all against it.'

In the end his pain and distress were decisive. Instead of going into the mountains, he went down the Rhine valley, reached Schaffhausen seven hours later, and returned to Basel (1342:391-495).

17

Pope Adrian's Appeal to Erasmus

Adrian's character; Botzheim's warning; moderation

1522-1523: Basel

On December 1, 1522, three months after reaching Rome, Pope Adrian wrote to Erasmus, urging him to publish a decisive refutation of Luther's teachings. 'We have read and reread your letters to us with great satisfaction and delight, both because they came from you whom we have always valued highly for your outstanding erudition and because they gave evidence of the highest devotion to ourselves and to the religion we profess. One thing we cannot possibly deny. Not only we ourselves but all other men have long been greatly surprised that you have not yet brought your fertile pen to attack these new heresies. There is universal agreement that you are the one person for whom this task seems to have been reserved by heaven. You have great intellectual powers, extensive learning, and a readiness in writing such as no one else in living memory has enjoyed. Furthermore, you have great influence and popularity among those nations from which this evil took its rise. It is well known that from boyhood to the present time, through all the stages of your life, you have constantly enriched every subject you have touched on. What do you suppose men will think and say about you if they now see you holding back in a matter where you have an obligation to respond, especially since the vigour of your writing remains as great as ever and your judgment has gained in maturity? Many are convinced that, once the rumour is put about of your writing against them, Luther's party will collapse. As it is, some of them boast of you as their leader, maintaining that everything is done on your advice and that you would never keep silence unless you approved of what they write, seeing that even the very smallest blemishes of language are more than you can tolerate in Holy Scripture. But you will confront all these evils with little effort as soon as you direct the energy of your intellect against those who throw Christian charity into chaos. Once you have done this, we do not doubt that Luther's supporters will be moved by your eloquence, your lively reasoning, and most of all your authority, and will readily return to the flock of their Redeemer which they have basely deserted, led astray by an evil spirit. You can readily see what an encouragement this would be to us. Remembering as you must how much more inclined we were to mildness than to severity in the days when we enjoyed the delightful freedom of study and what was still private life, you ought to reckon that this mercifulness has not been weakened but increased by our pastoral office' (1324A:1-6, 20-27, 53-61, 74-100).

This letter took over six weeks to reach Erasmus, so he had not received it when he wrote to Adrian on December 22, 1522: 'Most blessed Father, I send you for the second time, by the public courier of the city of Basel, a token of my devotion to yourself and my active loyalty to your see.

Nothing can be more stormy than the times we live in. The world looks to you alone to restore tranquillity to the affairs of men. If your Holiness instructs me, I will make so bold as to give you an outline of my own proposal for putting an end to this evil. Not much is gained by suppressing it by brute force in such a way that it soon breaks out again. My view is that we must not allow private resentment to bring mischief on Christ's cause. We must maintain the authority of men only so far as will not compromise the authority of Jesus Christ. May his spirit guide your heart and all your undertakings towards the salvation of the world and the glory of God' (1329:1-28, 43-45).

On Christmas Day he wrote to Johann von Botzheim. 'A pope who from genuine principle forwards the business of Christ will have my support. Nor have I any doubt that, being old, a scholar, and a man with great experience of affairs, he will answer our expectations. If he should fail us in any way, I at least will not go in search of strife. Truth is a mighty unconquerable thing, but it must be deployed with a wisdom learned from the gospel. Think how slowly Christ revealed his teaching. Such is my hatred of dissension and love of concord that I fear, if it came to the point, I should abandon some portion of the truth sooner than disturb the peace' (1331:47-55, 23-26).

'From personal acquaintance I know the Pope's character and qualities well', he told the Bishop of Basel, 'nor do I doubt that he will set much to rights in the way the church behaves. He will lay down rules for what clerics can wear, he will not stand those who are openly criminal, and he will compel them to say mass frequently. All these things have their place as regards the outward appearance of religion. Whether the force of true piety is rooted in them, I am not sure. He will command universal obedience thanks to the authority of the Emperor. The cardinals, even those who at heart wish him ill, will hide their feelings and put up with him until he has established the authority of the Roman see, now somewhat decayed. After that he cannot live long and his successor will have things all his own way. I have of course no wish to abolish the primacy of the see of Rome, but I should wish to see it conducted on principles which will give a lead to all who strive after the religion of the gospels, just as for some centuries now the lessons to be learned openly from its example have been entirely contrary to the teaching of Christ' (1332:69-86). It is remarkable that so cautious a man, so resolute in hostility to Luther, should have dared to say such things.

Throughout January 1523 he was 'toiling continually at my researches, from which I never take a holiday' (1332:2-3). Even at this time of bitter conflict he got Froben to publish two major works, an edition of the writings of Hilary in the fourth century and his paraphrase of John's Gospel, to which he added a long and important preface: 'After this life, which for no man can last long, there follows a life which will never end, in which each man will face the inescapable sentence of an incorruptible judge and reap the crop he has sown here, nor will anyone escape the alternative of receiving for his good deeds a crown of eternal blessedness or for his evil deeds being handed over to the eternal punishment of hell fire. Nothing therefore can be more important than that heavenly philosophy which Christ himself delivered to us all, which alone can make us impregnable against this world, against the prince of this world, against the infection of vice, the sickness of sin, against lust, avarice, ambition, gluttony and anger.

When the moral standards of the age are so much corrupted and there are these great dissensions in men's thinking that now reduce all things to chaos, where can we better seek refuge than in that pearl of great price which is the gospel?' (1333:156-163, 233-252).

The preface to his edition of Hilary's works, a document of phenomenal learning, is also a sermon demanding obedience in daily life. 'We neglect those things without which no one has any hope of attaining salvation. Unless I pardon my brother's sins against me, God will not pardon my transgressions against Him. Unless I have a pure heart, I shall not see God. You will not escape perdition unless you see to it that you have the fruits of the Spirit, which are love, joy, peace, patience, kindness, goodness, forbearance, gentleness, faith, moderation, self-control and chastity' (1334:215-225). Here again he could not resist slipping in an allusion to the Pope. 'If someone diminishes the authority of the Roman pontiff, the error is called a schism, but why is no one disturbed when some men attribute too much to that authority?' (1334:645-8).

Meanwhile Johann von Botzheim had received Erasmus' Christmas Day letter and felt uneasy about it. On January 7 he wrote an admirable reply, still preserved in his handwriting in the University Library at Wroclaw in Poland. 'Your letter goes on record that you will support the Pope to the best of your power. There is nothing absurd about this, provided the real truth is not suppressed. To hate dissension and love concord is evidence of genuine piety. But if the occasion should ever arise when you would rather abandon the cause of truth than provoke a breach of that concord, remember that truth must not be sacrificed to any and every objective. Truth must sometimes be maintained and not abandoned or hushed up in a way which might seem to be giving support to its opposite, something I would think one ought not to do on any pretext whatever. Nor will the truth, stated in the very moderate language which is habitual with you, be judged subversive by any who are good Christians at heart. It is impossible for you to reconcile convictions as violent and controversial as they are on this subject by peaceful agreement between the parties. I am much more afraid that, if you support the papal case in your desire to maintain concord, you will be encouraging greater danger and confusion. It is right that truth should win the day. It is right to be on the side of truth. I know your natural disposition in this regard. You would like to preserve truth entirely intact, if no one were hurt by it, which rarely or never happens. If the truth, which means Christ, is deserted to please men, this might lead to the extinction of truth on the ground that there are people who will find in it a pretext for subversion. Surely passions must give way on both sides and we must fix our eyes on Christ, who is the just judge. I know you are marvellously skilled in this art. Our age has never seen anyone to match you, who know so well with what skill one must write on dangerous topics. One must not attach too much importance to bishops and their tyranny, unless one is willing to contemplate the risk of bloodshed. This is a plague which spreads from the top downwards. If some cure could be applied to the head, the body and limbs would easily be restored to health' (1335:7-47).

Much as Erasmus needed these warnings, in reply he merely defended his own demands for reform and reiterated misgivings over the movement initiated by Luther. 'Has anyone been a more active opponent in print of putting one's trust in ceremonies, of superstitions concerning food and liturgy and prayer, of giving more weight to human inventions than to Holy Scripture and the commandments of God, of putting more trust in the saints than in Christ himself, and of the rash practice of laying down rules for every mortal thing? My misdeeds amount to this, that I am all for moderation and the reason why I have a bad name with both sides is that I exhort both to adopt a more peaceable policy. I have no objection to freedom if it is seasoned with charity, but scurrility can produce nothing but sedition and bloodshed. I merely wish to see what is now done in a subversive spirit done without subversion. I do not restrain those who wish to put out the fire; but I do condemn those who pour oil on the flames and are in a great hurry to remove by violent drugs a disease which has by now grown chronic over a thousand years and more, to the very great peril of the whole body. The apostles showed toleration to the Jews, who could not be weaned away from their ingrained taste for the Law; and the same, I believe, they would rightly show to these men who for so many centuries have accepted the authority of all those councils and popes and distinguished teachers, and find some difficulty in swallowing the new wine of the modern teaching. For the time being I assume that one party is wrong and the other entirely right in what they maintain. Let both sides pursue Christ's business on Christian principles' (1341A:1132-1180).

On January 23, 1523 Adrian replied to Erasmus' suggestion of outlining in a secret letter his proposal for putting an end to the 'terrible plague' brought about by Luther. 'Since many thousands of souls redeemed by the blood of Christ are being dragged straight to perdition', wrote the Pope, 'the greater the speed and secrecy with which you can expound to us your policy, the greater the service you can render to God. Speed is required by the common danger, secrecy by the danger to yourself, whose safety we value as we would our own'. Alluding to 'our common country, the studies and way of life which we both share, and the varied gifts of mind and character which the giver of all good things has lodged within you', Adrian urgently requested him 'to come to us, and to come quickly, and we will take all possible steps to see that you have no reason to repent of your journey and your toil, nor is there any reason why you should postpone your coming, for the winter has already started to recede and the danger of infection from the plague become almost non-existent' (1338:38-67).

It was March 22, 1523 before Erasmus was able to answer. 'Most holy Father, the bearer of this seemed to me more or less reliable, but he presented himself unexpectedly after dinner with the intention of setting out at first light next day. I nearly decided that it was wiser not to write at all on such a difficult subject than to write on the spur of the moment. None the less, your Holiness urges me so strongly and appeals to me almost as a matter of obedience to contribute any proposals I may have for bringing these disturbances to a peaceful end. I bow before your authority and write even at short notice, in hopes of writing more fully when I have more leisure and a more reliable bearer'.

Having stated firmly that 'no man shall read this letter except us two', he went on to explain that he was suffering so persistently from stone in the kidneys that he could not possibly travel over the snow-covered Alps to Rome. His excuse was genuine enough. He had nearly died on recent longer trips and he had had to return to Basel from Constance, but later on he admitted 'it was not really safe to trust Pope Adrian, however civil his language' (1496:64).

He explained to him, 'It is not only Germany that is in the grip of this movement: I would hardly dare to set down in how many regions and to what a depth the minds of ordinary people have been penetrated by support for Luther and hatred of the papacy'. He deplored the way he himself was being libelled in Rome and in Belgium as a heretic. 'Time was when hundreds of letters described me as the prince of the world of literature, the bulwark of a more genuine theology, but my popularity has cooled off or even turned into hatred. I wrote a great deal before suspecting that Luther had come into existence, almost all of it done in a hurry, for this is a congenital fault of mine' (1352:38-42, 105-107).

He suggested it was a great mistake to try 'to overwhelm this evil by severity and the knife, by imprisonment and scourging, by confiscation and exile, excommunication and death'. It would be better to 'offer pardon to those who have gone astray by some sort of destiny' (1352:168-198).

He proposed that 'the first thing to do will be to investigate the sources from which this evil springs up' and then that 'the world should be given some hope of changes in certain points where complaints of oppression are not unjustified, so far as it can be done without imperilling religion, while at the same time safeguarding the dignity of bishops'. Then he came to the crucial question.

'Your Holiness will ask, "What are these sources and what are the points that need reform?" To evaluate these my opinion is that, region by region, men should be called together who are incorruptible, influential, widely respected, emotionally well-balanced, whose opinion….' (1352:193-217).

But there the surviving text of the letter breaks off in the middle of a sentence, so after all we do not know what precise proposals Erasmus made.

18

Encouragement and Despair

Heretics burnt; Brunfels' accusation; Luther's tribute

1523-1524: Basel

Struggling with ill-health as he waited in Basel for the Pope's reply, Erasmus filled his days and nights revising previous publications and embarking on new ones. Cuthbert Tunstall, the Bishop of London, astonished that he had still not yet written a book against 'Luther's peculiar poison', urged him 'by the blood Christ shed to redeem the world and by the glory which you look for in heaven when your course in this life is run, to grapple with this hydra-headed monster who by abolishing the freedom of the human will makes God the only begetter of all wickedness, maintaining that everything happens according to fixed laws of necessity, so that it is not open to any man to act rightly even if he would' (1367:9, 18-22, 95-98). But from Strasbourg, Wolfgang Capito called upon him to do the opposite. 'You are set in the theatre of the world whether you will or no, and you must be and be seen to be a clear friend of the truth or a dissembler – such are the times now' (1374:69-71). Happily for him, there were still many who regarded him very highly. 'I shall live with my

Erasmus, as I always have hitherto', wrote a member of the Council of Flanders, 'every day, I mean, I shall spend some time among your brilliantly written books' (1373:11-14). And an unknown Italian, 'having bathed now and then in the deep waters of Aristotle and Plato', addressed Erasmus as 'the most thoroughbred champion of our Christian calling, the unchallenged leader of the whole world of literature in our generation', and gave thanks to God 'for producing such a man at this juncture, by whose incomparable labours the gospel field, smothered for so long with weeds and worthless tares, is hoed and weeded. As I read your works I have repeated to myself a hundred times those words, "I have found a man after my own heart"' (1372:22-58).

On April 23, 1523 he began work on a *Paraphrase of the Gospel of Luke*, an immense task, much the longest of all his paraphrases, yet in two months it was finished, complete with a substantial preface dedicating it to the 'Defender of the Catholic Faith', Henry VIII. 'First we are given a draught of faith', he explained to the King, 'which administers to the spirit a salutary shock of repentance. When that has laid us low, our sickness been driven out, and baptism left us emptied of our sins, anger is drawn off, gentleness and mildness instilled; generosity is substituted for greed, a passion for peace succeeds the love of fighting, and desire for the pleasures of the flesh is succeeded by desire for heavenly things. The Lord Jesus exhorts men to eat his flesh and to drink his blood, thinking of his teaching, which like bread makes the spirit active and robust, and like wine intoxicates it until it despises this life.' He surveyed the amazing impact of the gospel upon huge numbers of people who, abandoning the religion of their fathers, 'gave up the pleasures and vices to which they had been accustomed since the cradle' in favour of 'a sort of humble philosophy, for they all began to sing the same song, exalting Jesus Christ, the only Lord and Saviour of the world' (1381:209-302). He boldly informed the King, 'I have learned from my own experience that there is little profit in the Gospel if one's reading of it is perfunctory, but he who grows familiar with it by continuous careful thought will find a power in it that is in no other books. All Holy Scripture has a healing power, yet there is no drug in it more powerful than the Gospels' (1381:427-421, 256-258).

When the exposition was completed, Erasmus became gravely ill yet again. 'In July I suffered from the stone so long and severely that I had no hope of survival' (1422:20). He told Pirckheimer, 'I felt at heart a kind of happiness at the prospect of departing from this most unruly world to be with Christ. These troubles over Luther get worse every day and I see no way out. I had good hopes of our present Pope, but now I fear he may let me down. I wrote him privately a long letter with the greatest freedom, but he does not answer and I fear he may be offended. But I am withdrawing from these conflicts in favour of more peaceful pursuits. As I work on my paraphrases I seem to myself to become a better man' (1376:4-11, 1434:41, 1384:25-29).

On August 30, 1523 Froben published the book. Erasmus at once sent King Henry a sample copy. 'Here is Luke the physician, who has the secret of eternal life' (1385:12). The very next day was the first anniversary of Adrian's coronation in Rome, but the Dutch Pope was already seriously ill, worn out by the responsibilities and frustrations of his office, trying in vain to make peace between the Germans and the French, to unify Christendom in resistance to the Turks, to destroy Luther, and to rectify gross abuses in the Church. Though he kept struggling back to his desk, nothing could save him, and he died on September 14, only eighteen months after his election. Before Erasmus knew this, he learnt that two young friars had been burnt as Lutheran heretics by the Inquisition in Brussels. 'Whether I ought to deplore their deaths or not, I do not know', he wrote to Zwingli. 'At any rate, they died with exemplary and unheard-of determination, not for the articles of the faith but for Luther's paradoxes, for which I should not be willing to die myself, because I do not understand them. Luther puts forward a number of riddles which are on the face of it absurd: that "all the works of the saints are sin"; that "free will is mere words"; that "man is justified by faith alone and works are nothing to the point". To argue about how Luther wishes these things to be understood brings no profit that I can see. I am under the impression that I have maintained almost all that Luther maintains, only abstaining from riddles and paradoxes' (1384:4-16, 95-97). And, in spite of the burnings in Brussels, he reiterated, 'I shall remain steadfastly in the Catholic camp, upholding the cause of truth. I always have been and always shall be the most complete stranger to Luther's faction' (1386:60, 45, 7).

In December a young German named Otto Brunfels, who had abandoned his monastery and been attracted by Luther, wrote to Erasmus. 'I cannot describe the all-consuming anger I felt that you had taken refuge in the enemy camp' (1406:91-92). Knowing he spoke for a great many of his contemporaries, he did not mince his words: 'Long enough have we looked up to you and with good reason. You were the agent of our salvation. We were barbarians, fierce and untameable, and you civilised us. You showed the way by which we could end up not only educated but religious. But when you saw many men taking that path, some of whom were to wrest the victory from you in this field, whether you were overcome by pride, corrupted by bribes, or blinded by jealousy (as some suppose), instead of the old honey, or mixed in with it, you drip poison, and in the end like a scorpion plunge in your sting. Had you not done this, there is not a man to this day who would not reverence you, not one who would not share your successes, sing your praises, greet you with honour and respect. But when by your own behaviour you tarnish the record of your eloquence and darken the brightness of your own reputation, who can look up to you, who will respect you? You sin against your own soul. It is a most bitter grief to me that you should have come to such a pass, and that a man like myself, of no account and no learning, should have to do battle with you. Would that you, who ought now to be Christ's mouthpiece, had not sunk to such depths of insanity that you have become the head of those who have conspired against the Lord, the enemies of the gospel. For though you never openly attack it, you wrap things up and slip things in with extraordinary inconsistency, until all is confusion. You try simultaneously to establish both the papacy and the gospel, wheat and chaff together, darkness and light. What other purpose have you except utterly to overthrow all that you once founded, championed, and spread far and wide? No two things today have so little in common as Christ and pope, Rome and the church of Christ. At the same time you add this further point that there is too much bitterness in some of the things we do and that even we ourselves are not perfect. It is indeed a pretty saying of yours that mildness is the way to handle the gospel. Yes indeed, when concerned with the infirm, with those whose faith is weak, with such as need milk, but not when dealing with the stubborn and stiff-necked, the abandoned, the shameless and the hardened, who stop up their ears that they may not hear. If Luther, for instance, says some rather angry things about bishops and monks, there is no cruelty in this. It is demanded by their hardness of heart, their wickedness and their obstinacy – just as I too am rather free in speaking to you now. Repent, repent, I beg you in the name of Jesus Christ. Remember you are old, remember your vocation and the grace that was given you before so many witnesses. Fight for the gospel with all your might. There is no disgrace, no loss of face, in making good your escape. Only, you must act!' (1406:167-275). Three months later Erasmus admitted, 'I have not yet answered. I think it wiser to ignore him' (1432:55-56).

He revealed his despair to a diplomat in the Emperor's service. 'I am almost tired of life, as I watch the world's two most powerful kings, Charles V and Francis I, locked for so many years now in mortal conflict. Then there is another split almost more incurable, that between the new gospel and the old, an evil which daily grows and spreads more widely.' Happily he had had some good advice from Botzheim – 'you must continue to be your true self, a quiet, peacemaking writer of paraphrases' (1401:27-28) – on which he acted. 'I decided to steer clear of both camps, as I saw things I disliked in each, beseeching Christ the Almighty that he would one day turn this tempest of ours into tranquillity. Even so, I did not entirely abandon my researches, but concentrated on subjects which should give no great offense to either party, for besides many other things I have completed all the paraphrases on the New Testament except the Apocalypse. For some time this policy worked well enough, but now stones are thrown at me by both sides. Some of the champions of this new gospel are so crazy that Luther himself is compelled to attack them in print. My old age has coincided with these upheavals. Personally I think that death would be more tolerable than what I have to put up with. Had I known the stage this conspiracy had reached, I would rather have gone to live among the Turks than move here to Basel. How different was the verdict passed on my books by Pope Adrian, who laid under a ban of silence the theologians who were tirading against me' (1432:14-30, 1433:13-17).

Early in 1524 Erasmus was in touch with Clement VII who had succeeded Adrian, dedicating to him the paraphrase of Acts and sending him a sample copy. 'I pray, most holy Father, that it may be the will of the Lord Jesus to make you the founder of a new golden age. Such is the fervent wish of all of us who rightly detest our present divisions', which he thought could be ended if only Clement 'inspired hopes that you are willing to make certain changes which can be made without prejudice to true religion' (1418:68-77). He learned that the Pope had been delighted by the book, not only getting it nicely bound but 'desiring to have your advice and assistance near at hand' (1442:14-15). Erasmus was pleased. 'I only wish I could be in Rome. I know there is good reason for being there, but in my present condition I can hardly keep alive in my own room' (1424:23-27). Yet in April, attracted by 'the good weather and the fresh beauty of the world in springtime', he accepted pressing invitations to visit Besançon, seventy miles away in France, 'to rub off the staleness I have acquired by doing nothing and lying hidden for so long' (1440:5-6). Having survived 'many hours on horseback in intense heat', he was lavishly entertained. 'The magistrates wanted to organise a great banquet in my honour, had I not protested that I was critically ill.' Fever forced him to refuse all invitations. He could not even talk to the friends who had invited him. 'For several days I had my food in the bedroom. Lunch consisted of an egg and a small helping of chicken, cut very fine. Instead of wine, I had water warmed with sugar.' So he ordered his two servants to get the horses ready again. 'I did not want to remain in bed there and be a nuisance to people I did not know. I was sure the illness would last a long time, as it usually does' (1610:78-107).

On his return to Basel he heard from Luther again. 'Grace and peace from our Lord Jesus Christ. I have now been silent for some little time, good friend Erasmus, and though I expected that you as the older and more eminent of us would break silence first, yet after waiting in vain for so long, I am I think obliged by charity to make the first move. In the first place, I have no wish to complain if you have kept your distance from me in order to be quite free and uncommitted in opposing my enemies, the papists. Nor did I take it much amiss when in some passages in your published work, in order to secure their good will or appease their fury, you have attacked me and criticized me with some bitterness. When I perceive that the Lord has not yet given you the courage, or even the common sense, to join with me in a free and confident confrontation with those monsters I suffer from, I am not the man to dare to demand from you something beyond your powers and limitations. In fact I have put up with your weakness and respected it, and the measure of the gift of God in you. For the extent to which learning flourishes through you and wins the day, thus opening the way to the genuine study of the Bible, is a thing the whole world simply cannot deny, nor that there is a great and special gift of God in you for which we must all give thanks. And so I for my part have never wished to see you abandon or neglect the measure given you and involve yourself in our camp; for though with your abilities and your eloquence you could do great service to the cause, yet as your heart would not be in it, it would be safer to serve within your own gift. The one thing to be afraid of was that you might be persuaded by my enemies to attack my opinions in your published work, and that I should then be obliged to resist you to your face' (1443:1-25).

Luther admitted, 'Christ is my witness how sincerely I sympathise with you as the target of so much hatred and passion', but he suggested Erasmus' words had been so 'provocative, bitter and wounding' that indignation was understandable. 'How easy it is to write about modesty and yet how very difficult it is to be modest oneself, except by some special gift of the Spirit. Things have reached a stage at which there is very little to fear for our cause even if you oppose it with all your power, and still less if you sting here and there sometimes and show your teeth. Feeling is very bitter on both sides. What shall I do? Were it possible I should wish to act as mediator, that people might cease to attack you so fiercely and might allow you in your old age peacefully to fall asleep in the Lord. They would certainly do so if they took thought for your weakness and considered how great are the issues at stake, which have long since exceeded your capacity' (1443:29-32, 54-62).

Erasmus told Pirckheimer, 'Martin Luther has written

to me quite a civil letter, but I did not dare send an equally civil answer, for fear of those who distort everything' (1466:19-21). His hastily written reply started with the words, 'Cordial greetings. No, I do not concede that your passion for the purity of the gospel is more sincere than my own', and went on to say, 'when I look at certain passages in your work, I am much afraid that Satan is using his wiles to lead you astray, but there are other passages which so delight me that I wish my fears were groundless.' (1445:1-9).

Though this struggle was such a distress to him, Erasmus' mind was refreshed by his share in Froben's great edition of Jerome's writings. 'My experiences as I reread Jerome's works are much as one has when looking at pictures. A picture of moderate quality is quite attractive on first inspection, but if you study it more often, more closely, and more at leisure, it gradually loses its attraction. On the other hand, a painting by a distinguished artist becomes more and more admirable the more often and attentively you look at it. Jerome was a favourite in my adolescence, he was a favourite when I reached man's estate, but never have I enjoyed him more than during this rereading' (1451:149-156).

One may also hope he was refreshed by the news from Juan Luis Vives. 'On May 26 I bowed my neck under the yoke of matrimony and do not yet feel it at all heavy or the sort of thing I should like to shake off, but the outcome is in God's hands'. He was thirty-two years old, the bride nineteen. 'So far I have no reason to complain and all those who know us are delighted. They say nothing has happened here for years that has won such universal approval' (1455:7-11).

19

A Discussion of Free Will

God's will and man's will; God's justice and mercy

1524: Basel

Erasmus was right in thinking his reply to Luther had been less civil than Luther's letter, with its tribute to how his learning had 'opened the way to the genuine study of the Bible' (1443:15-19). Yet he was again taken to task, this time from Dresden, for still not having actually written against Luther. 'How much easier it would have been to extinguish a fire that was just breaking into flame than trying to put it out now when it has grown into such a vast conflagration! The blame for this, to speak my mind freely, falls in the first place on you. If only, while the times pointed that way and this plague had not yet claimed so many victims, you had adopted the attitude towards Luther which you now display and had descended into the arena and there played the part of a committed combatant, there would be no reason for our present troubles. However, since your method of fighting him hitherto has been never to declare open war but only to attack from a concealed position – a very light attack, almost as though you deliberately did not wish to hit him – the public have come to quite a different conclusion. Some have decided that you are an enemy of Luther and some that you are in collusion with him, pretending to differ but really in agreement. If you wish to be relieved of this misconception it will be absolutely essential to disclose yourself and come out at last into the open, proving to the world by an open confrontation with Luther what your opinions really are and at the same time defending the church from a most abominable heresy. Unless you do this, there will be a universal cry of protest that you have betrayed the supreme position of the church and paid no heed to the purity of the gospel or to your personal duty' (1448:42-63). This account of Erasmus was as accurate from a Catholic standpoint as that of Otto Brunfels from the reforming position.

And so at long last he began to work on what he called 'the first draft of a trifling piece about the freedom of the will, on which I have wasted five days and very tedious days they were, for I knew I was not engaged in my proper field' (1419:1-5). He sent a copy of this first draft to the professor of theology in Basel, asking him 'to run your eye over it and tell me where I have missed the whole target', and another copy with the same request to Henry VIII. He told Pope Clement, 'I am now engaged on a book on the freedom of the will in answer to Luther' (1418:58), while at the same time working towards a fourth edition of his Latin New Testament and collaborating with Froben in producing further volumes of the works of Jerome.

Yet he felt uncertain about the project, admitting to the Archbishop of Canterbury that he 'would gladly have avoided taking the field against the Lutherans' (1488:30) and telling Cardinal Wolsey that 'though encouraged by his serene Majesty and yourself, it is a rash thing to do in Germany as conditions are now, likely to excite very serious opposition' (1486:2-5, 1487:5). In his heart of hearts he knew 'I am operating in a field that is not mine' (1483:4).

In spite of his misgivings, *A Discussion of Free Will* was published by Froben in September 1524. 'I treat the subject with such moderation that I know Luther himself will not take offense' (1466:66-67). It was not the decisive attack Catholics had expected, for it made no reference to Luther's break with the Papacy or the reforms he had initiated. 'So that no one interprets it as a fight between two gladiators, I take issue solely with this one teaching of Luther, and the debate is carried on without abuse, because this is more seemly for Christians' (CWE. Vol. 76. pp. 6-7).

In the eighty-five pages which followed, Erasmus repeatedly stated the opinions he was concerned to refute, such as that free will is a fiction, an empty term; that free will can do nothing but sin; that all our actions, whether good or bad, are performed in us by God regardless of our will, so that whatever we do happens not by free will but by absolute necessity; that God rewards his own good works in us and punishes his evil works in us; that all God's commands are impossible for us to fulfil; that even after receiving grace man does nothing except sin; and that all works which do not proceed out of love of God, however morally good they may be, are no less detestable to God than adultery and murder. But he began by explaining what he suspected was perhaps more important than the discussion itself. 'There are certain things of which God intended us to be entirely ignorant, such as the day of our death and the time of the Last Judgment. There are certain things he intended us to examine so that we might venerate him in mystical silence, places in Holy Scripture whose ambiguity no one has clearly solved. There are certain other things he intended to be perfectly clear to us, such as the precepts for a good life, which should be learned by everyone. And there are some secret places in Holy Scripture into which God did not intend us to penetrate very far, and if we attempt to do so, the further in we go the less clearly we see' (pp.8-10).

He admitted 'there are many passages in Holy Scripture which seem to support the freedom of the human will and some which seem to deny it completely' (p.21), but so far as he knew 'from the apostles' time to this day there has not been a single Christian writer who has completely denied the power of free will' (p.15). Then he launched into a review of hundreds of verses in both Old and New Testaments bearing upon the question.

He quoted such Old Testament passages as 'I have set before you life and death, blessings and curses: now choose life' (Deut. 30:19) and 'If you are willing and obedient you will eat the best from the land, but if you resist and rebel, you will be devoured by the sword' (Is. 1:19-20), arguing that 'it would be ridiculous for God to tell someone to choose if it were not in his power to turn one way or the other'. He maintained that 'if the human will is in no sense free to do good or evil, it would have been more suitable for God to say "if I am willing" than "if you are willing" and "if I am unwilling" than "if you refuse".' There seemed little point in further quotations of this kind when 'all Holy Scripture is full of such exhortations, which are meaningless if doing good or evil is a matter of necessity' (pp.34-37).

Then he turned to the New Testament. 'We find Christ saying "If anyone wants to come after me, let him deny himself" and "if you want to enter life, keep the commandments", but how on earth could you say "if you want to" to someone whose will was not free? Is not his teaching full of exhortations such as "come unto me, take my yoke upon you and learn from me", "seek and you will find", "watch and pray"? All these, as well as the warnings and threats in the Gospels would be meaningless or superfluous if everything is referred to necessity' (pp.40-41). And he had no problem in pointing out that our free will is assumed throughout the Epistles of Peter and Paul in countless appeals to 'fight the good fight', 'cast off the works of darkness', 'put off your old self and put on your new self', 'make every effort to add to your faith virtue'. 'I find difficulty in reconciling such terms with a will that does nothing, but is merely passive. What is the meaning of the constant praise of obedience to God, if we are tools for good works as well as bad, like an axe in the hands of a carpenter?' (pp.43, 45).

'Now it is time to look at the other side of the question and consider scriptural passages that seem to deny free will completely.' He quoted Romans 9:18, 'God has mercy on whom he wants to have mercy and hardens whom he wants to harden', confessing that 'it seems absurd that God, who is good as well as just, should be said to have hardened a man's heart to illustrate his own power through that man's evil'. His understanding was that 'God's lenient toleration of the sinner leads some to repentance and makes others more persistent in their wrongdoing. So God has mercy on those who acknowledge his goodness and amend their ways, but the hearts of those who have been given a chance to repent, but disdain his goodness and go on to do worse, are hardened.' He suggested that 'God hardened Pharaoh's heart' in Exodus should be understood in the same sense as 'God gave them over to a depraved mind' in Romans 1:28; it was punishment for sin (pp.46-52).

'Admittedly the problem of God's will and predestination is difficult, for since God's will is the principal cause of everything that happens it does seem to impose necessity on our will. Paul does not resolve this problem, he simply rebukes anyone who would debate it, but it is the godless protester he rebukes. He would give a different answer to the well-meaning person who asked why something happens. The statement that God loved Jacob and hated Esau in Romans 9:13 does not actually refer to human salvation. If you insist on the literal sense, God does not love or hate in the way we do: the prophet is not speaking here of the hatred by which we are eternally damned but of temporal affliction' (pp. 46-49).

One by one he dealt with other biblical passages which seem to exclude human will, including 'Apart from me you can do nothing' and 'What have you, that you did not receive?' He suggested that the words, 'No one can come to me unless the Father who has sent me draws him' did not imply absolute necessity. God's drawing 'makes one want what one may still refuse' (p.66).

In Philippians 2:12-13 Paul says, 'Work out your own salvation with fear and trembling, for it is God who works in you to will and to act according to his good purpose'. 'This passage definitely teaches that both God and man work. If man does nothing, why say "work out"?' (pp.68-69).

1 Corinthians 15:10 reads 'By the grace of God I am what I am and his grace to me was not in vain. No, I worked harder than all of them, yet not I but the grace of God that

was with me'. 'He acknowledges God as the author, then recognises how human will strives alongside divine assistance. If Paul had not done anything, why did he say that he had? The point of the correction was not that we should think he had done nothing, but so that he should not seem to ascribe to his own powers what he had achieved with the help of God's grace' (pp.69-70 and 73).

Summing up, Erasmus maintained that the apparently contradictory biblical verses 'are easily reconciled if we join our will to God's grace' (p.58).

'Pelagius seemed to attribute too much to free will. Luther cut its throat and made away with it altogether. I favour the opinion of those who attribute something to free will but most to grace. Grace is the principal cause of our salvation, our will is the secondary cause, in that it does not resist the grace of God (pp. 79-80). If we accept this, it does not invalidate Luther's godly Christian assertions that we must put all our trust in God and his promises. Once the freedom of the will has been denied, I do not see how the problem of the justice and mercy of God can be resolved. How can God be just, let alone merciful, to condemn to eternal torment those in whom he has not seen fit to work good deeds? Would not such a person be justified in saying "Why punish me for a fault for which you are to blame?"' (pp.76-88).

In closing he explained why it is essential to attribute some responsibility to free will, in order 'to allow the ungodly, who have deliberately fallen short of the grace of God, to be deservedly condemned, to clear God of the false accusation of cruelty and injustice, to free us from despair, protect us from complacency, and spur us on to moral endeavour. For these reasons nearly everyone admits the existence of free will, but asserts that it can achieve nothing without the perpetual grace of God. Our mental capacity for judgment was darkened but not extinguished by sin. Just as our first parents' sin has been passed on to their offspring, so a tendency to sin has been transmitted to us all. Although the freedom of the will has been wounded by sin, it is not dead: although lamed, it has not been destroyed' (pp. 23-27 and 87).

On November 13 Juan Luis Vives wrote from London to tell Erasmus, 'Your book on the freedom of the will was handed to the King yesterday. He read several passages of it and says he will read it through. He is particularly delighted with the passage in which you discourage mortal men from exploring too intensely the secrets of the divine majesty. The queen too instructed me to send you her greetings' (1513:7-14).

20

Monstrous Evils; Monstrous Remedies

Pirckheimer's review; crazy Lutherans abused; violence

1524: Basel

While *A Discussion of Free Will* was being printed, Pirckheimer was writing another of his brilliant letters to Erasmus. 'I am sure Luther is not ill-disposed to you, my distinguished friend, although he can be venomous in his writings, but then you don't lack a barbed tongue yourself and there are many people who would like to embroil the two of you in a confrontation. It appears that you have settled some of your differences, which pleases me very much. I am certain that Luther will be true to his word, unless you are the first to raise the call to battle. If the enemies of truth could stir up both of you to a fight, there is nothing which would delight them more. I hope God and your friends will avert such a disaster. But I have never felt any confidence that the two parties could be reconciled. I know the Romans will make no concessions, none at least of any significance, for that would be contrary to the long tradition in which they have been formed. But it is very difficult to hoodwink the people any longer, for now their eyes are open and they know the truth. So these men are now trying what force can accomplish, since bluff has met with little success. On the other side there is no lack of persons who would prefer to settle the issue by blows rather than words. Sensible people who recognise that old ingrained habits cannot be eradicated in a single moment are now dismissed as smooth-tongued impostors by these troublemakers, who have made the freedom of the spirit an excuse for the sins of the flesh. Everyone can see the dangers that lie ahead, while the Romans maintain their stubborn attitude and try to defend their manifest errors, and the followers of the gospel (as they call themselves) want to demonstrate the truth in words rather than deeds. I have little doubt that much that is being done in the name of the gospel is displeasing to Luther. But what can he do if things do not always turn out as he hoped? We know what those false brethren did to the Apostle Paul while he was spreading the message of the true faith. There is no wheat without tares. Some will say Luther should have acted more moderately and ought to have foreseen what is happening everywhere. But, granted that he was not too experienced in the conduct of affairs and that he was deceived in his expectations, was this any reason for him to hold his tongue and refrain from proclaiming the truth? Is there anyone so foolish that he does not realize the schemes and tricks and evil designs of those who call themselves religious? It is true that they succeeded in covering up their faults: no one dared open his mouth, let alone reprove them for their sins. When have they ever made an effort to correct the errors in which they are ensnared? Is it any wonder that men cry out when, if they held their peace, not even the stones would be silent? Yet

I know how much could have been accomplished by a more moderate policy, indeed Luther himself is now aware of this. But how can one deal moderately with obstinate men who know nothing of moderation? Monstrous evils, so numerous as these, cannot be abolished without monstrous remedies. I feel bound to say these things, my dear Erasmus, because of my affection for you. I was hoping you would visit us some time, though you and I will never be far apart, however great the distance which separates us' (1480:21-132).

In contrast to this careful survey and to the restraint Erasmus had himself maintained in discussing free will, most of his surviving letters from this period are full of abuse of people who had been influenced by the movement for reform. It seemed to him essential to prove that he had never had anything to do with it, so he greatly reduced his criticisms of Catholicism and sharply increased his antagonism to everything Lutheran, though occasionally able to admit that 'when I survey the excessively corrupt life led by Christians everywhere, I should almost have judged Luther to be a necessary evil' (1522:13-15). While 'distressed at the extremism of Luther's views and his bitterness, equalled only by his arrogance' (1526:113-115), he reserved his strongest hostility for 'crazy Lutherans, characters whose excesses are offensive even to Luther himself, who have on their lips five words – gospel, God's word, faith, Christ, and Spirit – yet I see many among them who leave me in no doubt that they are moved by the spirit of Satan' (1489:26, 1488:17-18, 1483:8-10). It has to be remembered that in the new freedom of thought, to which both Erasmus and Luther had contributed so substantially, wild ideas also proliferated. Once long established Catholic ways were challenged and abandoned, it was not easy to decide what should replace them. In this context Luther was comparatively moderate. There was no lack of other innovators, more extreme and undisciplined.

Erasmus' splendid work on the paraphrases of the Epistles, the Gospels, and the Acts of the Apostles was behind him, crowning his unique contribution to the study of the New Testament, and his mind was now taken up with the changes going on all around. 'No one would believe how widely the evil has spread and spreads every day, nor can I fail to see what friends I have lost and how may of them have turned into enemies. I wished at first that this split, which is more dangerous than many people realize, might be healed by a policy of moderation, but now I see that some of the ringleaders have no purpose in view but universal chaos. Thus mere necessity will compel the princes to restrain sedition by force' (1506:6-7, 21-25, 1512:37). He became intensely critical of people living close to him in Basel. 'What Luther is like as a person, I do not know. In these parts our new gospel provides us with a new sort of men: headstrong, impudent, deceitful, foul-mouthed, liars, scandalmongers, no good to anyone, a nuisance to all, subversive, crazy, noisy rascals. I dislike them so much that if I knew any city that was free of these gentry I would move there' (1522:95-100). Some were shocked to hear such unrelieved abuse from the man who had long been the champion of mildness, but he insisted that 'these pseudo-Lutherans despise Luther and will overthrow him unless some deity comes to the rescue; radicals as they are, they have the support of leaders like Capito, Oecolampadius, and Zwingli' (1498:8-10, 1497:17-18).

Yet he remained friendly with Luther's colleague, Philip Melanchthon. 'Your gifts have always inspired me with respect and affection', he told him on September 6, 1524. 'In fact, were not Wittenberg so far away, I should not have hesitated to come and spend a few days in your part of the world for an exchange of ideas with Luther and yourself' (1496:39, 17-19). In spite of such a pleasing start, the remaining two hundred lines of this letter are full of extravagant criticism. 'I know nothing of your church; at the very least it contains people who will, I fear, overturn the whole system. In the old days the church had its false apostles, but in our time they are lovingly supported by our gospel chiefs' (1496:66-76). He specially mentioned his former friend and colleague, Wolfgang Capito, who had become the leader of the Reformation in Strasbourg. 'Many people think very ill of him and I have some ugly suspicions; he always smelled like a rascal' (1496:120, 77). 'Oecolampadius is a little more restrained than the others. The friendship I once had with him has turned into an open quarrel, yet I must concede that he has considerable competence in theology and the three ancient tongues. No one thinks more highly of him than I do. He is an excellent man, but cannot accept advice' (1496:81, 1559:27-30, 1384:56-59). He repeatedly alluded to Otto Brunfels, who had called upon him to repent, as 'that scabby character' and described Guillaume Farel, who was becoming influential in western Switzerland, as 'the most poisonous liar I have ever seen: he has no control over what he says or writes' (1534:26-27, 1477A:6-7). He recoiled from having anything to do with such men. 'How can I convince myself that they are led by the spirit of Christ when their behaviour is so far from Christ's teaching? New hypocrites

I see, new tyrants, and not one grain of the spirit of the gospel. But there are some people who cry to heaven that the gospel is overthrown if anyone resists their own mad conduct' (1496:160-168, 220-222). At this stage in his life he was prone to describe those of whom he disapproved as mad, raving mad, lunatics, even as 'not human beings at all, but raging demons' (1445:66-67).

In its wisdom and restraint Melanchthon's reply was a great contrast. 'You are quite right, dear Erasmus, to complain of the behaviour of our modern professors of the gospel, who bark at a man of your importance, rouse the common people with subversive sermons, make violent attacks on learning and undermine the whole system of society. Luther is quite unlike them, but deeply concerned as he is at these abuses, he believes none the less that these scandals are stirred up by the devil in order to overwhelm the gospel somehow or other, so he thinks it his duty not to turn back or abandon the common cause. You on the other hand seem so deeply offended by the faults of some of these wretches that you take against the cause and the teaching too. You may perhaps think you are on the right lines, but I am afraid that such an attitude may prove a danger to the gospel, for you cannot deny that Luther's cause has taken to its heart the gospel teaching. So I do beg you, dear Erasmus, not to think that Luther is on the side of those whose character is rightly rejected and not to be prejudiced against his teaching by the folly of any individual. He detests cruelty, self-seeking, and all subversive policies, putting his life and reputation very much at risk by his opposition to a new faction of bloodthirsty teachers. You draw up a list in which you collect the greatest wretches in order to bracket them with

Oecolampadius and his like. Now what, I ask you, was the object of that?' (1500:1-39).

On December 10, 1524 Erasmus wrote again to Melanchthon. 'There is much in Luther's views which I find offensive. I dislike particularly the extraordinary vehemence with which he treats whatever doctrine he decides to defend and that he never stops until he is carried to extremes. To be honest, the general corruption of Christian morals called out for bitter reproof, but my preference was for a temperate frankness so that we might induce even bishops and rulers to share in the endeavour. What Luther has in mind I do not know. I wanted to reform the religious life of the priests without lessening their authority, and to aid good men who are now buried beneath the rituals of the monks without giving evil men an opportunity to sin more freely. I also hoped that things to which we had grown accustomed through long familiarity might be gradually corrected in such a way that we could avoid throwing everything into confusion. Whatever changes heaven may bring about, there will never be any shortage of things to complain about. Our problems can be mitigated but not removed completely. However many rivers flow into the sea, it always keeps its characteristic savour. And the remedy is sometimes worse than the disease. What could be more deadly than the present dissension? Is all this worth it, to have a church devoid of images and a few changes made in the rite of the mass? Is there anything which is less likely to foster Christian piety than for ordinary people to hear, and for young people to have it drummed into their ears, that the pope is Antichrist, that bishops and priests are demons, that the constitutions of men are heretical, that confession is a pernicious practice, that works, merit, human effort are heretical ideas, that there is no freedom of the will but all is governed by necessity, and that it makes no difference what a man performs? Some people spread such ideas abroad without qualifying them in any way, encouraged by men whom Luther embraces as the leading exponents of evangelical teaching. In imagining his ideal republic, Plato realized that people could not be governed without lies; far be it from a Christian to tell a lie, and yet it is not expedient to tell the whole truth to ordinary people. Luther has a fiery temperament: he has won such success, such widespread support, such general applause as would turn the head of even the most modest of men' (1523:28-38, 49-92, 180-185).

He was encouraged by reactions to *A Discussion of Free Will*. 'I have read your book', wrote the abbot of a monastery, 'and greatly prefer this balanced Erasmian view to the critical teaching of the Lutherans' (1525:20-22). But in Basel it was different. 'Here it has raised a storm. In every single sermon Oecolampadius produces some argument against it' (1526:243, 1522:93-94). And he was astonished to hear that in Cologne the Franciscans were saying 'Erasmus laid the egg and Luther hatched it', to which he retorted that 'the egg I laid was a hen's egg and Luther has hatched a chick of very, very different feather' (1528:15-18).

Then on December 12 he embarked on a careful review of the whole situation. 'It was largely the mad turmoil created by indulgence-sellers, whose profits seemed to be threatened, that fanned a tiny spark into such an immense conflagration. I hardly dare to trust my own judgment when I reflect on the thousands of supporters who favour Luther's cause, among whom – even discounting the sheer fact of numbers – I recognise many men of great ability, good judgment and uncommon learning, who had always seemed to me to lead virtuous and godly lives. I often wondered what they saw in Luther's work to make them receive it with such unswerving enthusiasm and cling to it so tenaciously. Sometimes the thought occurred to me that it was my own stupidity which prevented me from seeing what was crystal clear to them. So there is no reason why anyone should criticise me for being slow to act. I often felt sad at the extent to which Christian piety had declined. The world had become bewitched by ceremonial, evil monks reigned unchecked, theology had been reduced to subtle sophistries, while bishops and priests acted like tyrants in the name of the Roman pontiff. When I reflected on these things the thought came to me that it had pleased God to use Luther as once he used the Pharaohs, the Philistines, the Romans, and men like Nebuchadnezzar. For Luther's successes can hardly have come about without God's help. I came to the conclusion, therefore, that I should leave the outcome of this tragedy to Christ. All I could do was dissuade everyone I could from joining the sect' (1526:45-46, 116-148).

Since it was clear that the Catholic leaders 'had made up their mind to crush dissent with violence' he had to proceed cautiously. 'One could argue that it is right to send to the stake anyone who opposes an article of faith or any other doctrine which has been accepted by the general consent of the church, but it is not right to punish every error with the stake, unless the offense involves sedition or some crime for which the law prescribes the death penalty. What worries me now is that the common remedies, such as imprisonment, scourging, exile, confiscation, excommunication and the stake, will simply make the evil worse. Two men were burned at Brussels, and it was precisely at that moment that the city began to support Luther. If the infection had reached only a few, surgery of some sort might have been effective, but now it has become so widespread. Is anyone impressed by a recantation which has been extorted through terror of the stake?' (1526:158-183, 1499:34-35).

21

The Mind Active, The Body Tormented

The Archbishop; Toussain; Plutarch; Chrysostom

1525: Basel

On January 30, 1525 Erasmus Schets, a merchant-banker in Antwerp, wrote to him for the first time. 'My name is Erasmus, but I am a very different Erasmus from you. You, and you alone, are the great Erasmus and there is no one with whom you can be compared. Your Paraphrases with their immense learning have brought the wisdom of heaven and the message of the gospel within range of our human frailty. Now whoever wishes to read these works will find himself drawn from darkness into light, from weariness to rest, from the burden and stain of sin to freedom and purity of heart. Who would not rejoice in that noble mind of yours which has brought forth such things for us? When, under the guidance of the Spirit we embrace this religion in faith and hope, we are seized with a burning love of God and are carried into paths of righteousness, set free and made strangers to every evil thought and to all those troubles which prey upon our age. But there is something else which I cannot pass over. My friends in Spain tell me how much you are talked about and that princes, scholars and persons of repute think so highly of you that on points of doctrine and on Scripture they consider nothing worth reading except what you have written. They regard you as someone unique in the world' (1541:1-24, 35-45).

In reply, Erasmus had a suggestion to make. 'I receive an annuity from the Archbishop of Canterbury, but I lose heavily on it, partly because of the rate of exchange, partly because of the charges made by the bankers. I am sure you have business connections in England. So if, with the help of acquaintances of yours, you could arrange for my pension to reach me with fewer deductions, I should be most grateful' (1583:2-7). The outcome was that Schets advised the Archbishop to deposit the money with a Spaniard living in London, 'who quickly agreed, saying he would be delighted to have the opportunity of serving you, as you are rightly considered a giant among men' (1647:8-10). Schets' agents then delivered the money to him in Basel.

With the publication of his study on free will, mild as it was, the breach between Erasmus and Luther was complete. 'Lutherans regard me as an enemy: I am battling against all the followers of Luther, with no prospect of a truce' (1559:23, 1608:47). Time and again he reiterated his convictions. 'I consider myself a Catholic: in attempting to change everything, Luther is destroying everything' (1596:53, 1597:8-9). Yet Catholics remained unconvinced. 'My words still fall on deaf ears. Anyone who wants to see pontiffs, bishops, priests and monks better than they are at present is just about branded a Lutheran. No matter what I do, I am still considered a Lutheran and continue to be the target of vicious pamphlets' (1566:21-23, 1624:42-44). Whatever he said against Luther, 'the other side, far from giving an inch, tightens the old chains more tightly everyday' (1653:24) and was not impressed by his insistence that 'the original source of this disaster was the blatantly godless lives of some of the clergy' (1634:96-97).

But he took the risk of writing to the Cardinal Bishop of Metz on behalf of Pierre Toussain, a youth who had taken refuge in Basel after being refused permission to preach in France and had actually boarded with Oecolampadius. 'Although I have had many frank conversations with him, I have never detected a hint of sympathy on his part for those whose opinions are condemned by the Roman pontiff. If he continues in his studies as he has begun, he will be a great asset to the whole country. How rare it is to see a young man turning aside from all the pleasures which his contemporaries pursue so madly, poring night and day over the noblest authors and finding his greatest delight not in girls and drink and dice, but in the sacred texts. It is priests like this whom we need today, not men who impose their faith on others by imprisonment and threats of violence, but who follow St. Peter's advice and trust to the power of persuasion, being ready at all times to give an answer to any man who asks. Otherwise, is there any difference between a priest and a murderous bully? The world now detest priests because of their ignorance of Holy Scripture and their enslavement to lust, extravagance and money, but it will begin to love and respect them when they change their ways and become learned, chaste, sober and generous. For the moment I should like to appeal to your Eminence to help a young man who deserves every consideration and whom you will one day be glad to have rescued' (1559:18-20, 56-66, 116-

120). Toussain was to spend most of his long life in the service of the Reformation.

In April 1525 Froben published Erasmus' translations of two moral treatises by Plutarch, *On Anger* – 'which is intense among the young because of their hot blood and takes on a new vigour among the old because of the infirmities of age' – and *On Inquisitiveness* – 'which has been given to children to inspire them with a thirst for knowledge and to the old as a remedy for apathy and depression, or as a defence against fraud'. Erasmus dedicated the book, which included the original Greek texts, in a revealing statement addressed to the treasurer of the King of Hungary. 'I have perused these volumes with some care in the past, but I feel I have derived considerable profit from reading them more carefully and examining them in greater detail. Socrates brought philosophy down from heaven to earth. Plutarch brought it into the privacy of the home and into the study and the bedroom of the individual. This is a field which interests me more these days, because things have reached such a state of confusion throughout the Christian world that it is hardly safe to speak of Christ, whether what one says is true or false. Under every stone there sleeps a scorpion. The subjects which Plutarch discusses in these essays are such as anyone at any time would find immediately applicable to the ordinary concerns of life' (1572:69-88).

And only a month later he had completed a much improved edition of the original Greek text of *The Priesthood*, a major work by Chrysostom, Bishop of Constantinople in the fourth century. 'Here is an offering from Froben and myself', he said in dedicating it to Pirckheimer. 'He has covered the costs; I have given my time to the text. I am writing for the young, and this volume reads like the work of a young man. He discusses with remarkable eloquence the dangers which beset those who seek the office of a priest, and how difficult it is for a bishop to carry out his duties properly' (1558:186-189, 279-292).

For many years he had repeatedly suffered from kidney stones and 1525 was no exception. 'I wage a perpetual war against the stone, which keeps up such a fierce assault upon this poor fragile frame of mine that those who have to face death only once seem to me the most fortunate of men. But the Lord knows what is best for each of us and gives us the strength we need. The pain is torture. With its cruel escort it moves from the back through the abdomen to the region of the spleen, only to burst forth into the bladder, causing injury and distress wherever it goes. I use a remedy for which Thomas Linacre, chief physician to the King of England, was responsible. I was shy about asking for his help, but no one could have been more attentive. A druggist was called. The medication was heated in my bedroom and applied in the presence of the doctor himself. It never failed me till this last attack, which came on without warning, though a general feeling of anxiety and depression warned me that trouble was brewing. It was so severe that I began to hope for an end to my miseries. I was in labour for fully ten days and then, when I had given up all hope of being rid of the thing, I brought forth a huge stone. It is not that I am tired of this life, but like Paul I should like to be free and be with Christ. Even now my recovery is slow, if it can be called recovery to be spared for new tortures and to face death again and again' (1543:16-17, 1548:3-5, 1554:6-11, 1558:78-102).

Such experiences raised other problems in his mind.

'Since man, being composed of body and soul, is troubled by two kinds of affliction, wise men have always sought to know whether the ailments of the body or those of the soul are worse, and the answer they have given is that ailments of the soul have more terrible consequences. Yet common opinion is far from agreeing and we cannot be surprised that those who put the body before the soul also make inverted judgments about what is good and what is bad. Antiquity counted some three hundred varieties of disease; to this number new and previously unknown diseases have been added and continue to be added every day in a sort of guerrilla war against the science of medicine. But who could count the ailments of the soul? I wish it were only in numbers that they surpassed the ills of the body, but they have the advantage in many other respects as well. In the first place it is the better part of us which they harm. Physical illnesses only make men sick, but diseases of the soul make us evil and wretched as well. Moral failings – rampant lust, immersion in self-love, the craving for money, envy, or abominable desires – not only cause mental torment but are generally accompanied by physical problems too. They rob the mind of its calm and bring shame to the sufferer. The man whose feet are crippled with gout is still sound in eye and ear, but a single moral ailment corrupts the whole mind, for there is no moral sickness which does not bring with it a whole regiment of vices. Plagues of the mind spare neither rank nor sex nor age: they are restrained by no boundaries but sweep the earth with unimaginable speed: once they have set in, it is not easy to be rid of them' (1593:23-49, 70-75). Then he wondered which physical affliction was the worst. 'In my opinion the prize will fall easily to that disease of unknown origin which has stalked every region of the earth for many years now, though there is no settled convention about its name. Most men call it the French, but some the Spanish pox. Is there any plague which has traversed the various regions of Europe, Asia and Africa with equal speed? Does any penetrate more deeply into our veins and organs, or persist more doggedly, or defy more stubbornly the skill and treatment of the doctors? Is there any disease more contagious or responsible for more cruel torments?' (1593:93-101).

22

One of the Wonders of the World

Marguerite; the Eucharist; Louis de Berquin

1525: Basel

On September 28, 1525 Erasmus wrote to a woman, to Marguerite of Angoulême, the sister of King Francis, at that time a prisoner of war in Spain. She was widely admired for her learning, her grasp of several languages, her patronage of authors, her devotion to her brother, and her unselfish care for others. She had befriended Pierre Toussain, who probably took the letter to her. Her husband and her sister-in-law had both died recently. Knowing that she was 'buffeted by such a storm of trouble' gave Erasmus the chance to address her. 'I have long admired the many splendid gifts with which God has endowed you: learning of which even a philosopher might be proud, chastity, self-control, a devout nature, an indomitable strength of will, and a remarkable contempt for all transient things. Who would not admire such qualities in the sister of a mighty king, qualities which are rarely to be found among priests and monks? I would not mention these things if I were not certain that you impute nothing to your own strength, but ascribe all praise to the Lord, who is the giver of every good gift. I know how bitter is the disaster which has befallen you, but in this world nothing is so terrible that it can shake a soul whose anchor is truly fixed on that immovable rock, which is Christ Jesus. I do not flatter you because of your position. I cannot help but revere in the Lord such a brave and noble woman as yourself. I praise and esteem you for what I know you to be. May the Lord Jesus keep you safe and make you abound in him with the true riches of his blessing' (1615:10-34, 69-70).

It was during 1525 that Erasmus' correspondence revealed the intense theological debate about the Eucharist aroused by Luther's resistance to Catholic tradition. A letter from Botzheim vividly described what was happening. 'I see many sects springing up, even among those who glory in the one gospel. To what extent this is Christ's will is a question I leave to others to decide. I shall not listen to any of these people or take any notice of what they say, for I am content with my own simple faith in Christ. I do not intend to torture myself trying to puzzle out which of them has the finer arguments. There are so many theories to explain what takes place when we partake of the body and blood of our Lord. One man holds it is merely a commemoration and wishes it to be administered by officers of the state. Another angrily protests that beneath the elements lie the real body and blood of our Lord, just as they were when Christ was on the cross, and insists the sacrament must be administered by a priest. One man wishes to hold the elements in his own hands, another to receive them from the hands of a priest. One is satisfied to communicate in one kind, another fights like a gladiator for both kinds. One wishes to receive the blood from a silver chalice, another from a cup made of pine or ash. One wants the bread which has always been used for this purpose, but another, not wishing to seem deficient in imagination, introduces some new kind of wafer' (1574:8-26).

Alongside Erasmus in Basel yet another view was rapidly becoming dominant. 'A new doctrine has raised its head, that there is nothing in the Eucharist except bread and wine. This heresy has caught on everywhere. Oecolampadius, preaching it here day after day, has made the notion difficult to refute by buttressing it with so much evidence and such an imposing structure of argument that, unless God prevents it, even the elect are likely to be led astray. His book on the subject is so learned, well-written, and thorough, that anyone who wishes to answer him will have his work cut out. I would also judge it pious, if anything could be so described which is at variance with the general opinion of the church, from which I consider it perilous to dissent' (1618:9-13, 1620:97-99, 1624:36-40, 1621:25, 27, 1636:3-6). Indeed, this had become his guiding principle: to shun what was perilous and to accept the general Catholic opinion. 'Hitherto, along with all other Christians, I have always worshipped in the Eucharist the Christ who suffered for me and I see no reason now to change my views. No human argument could make me abandon what is the universal teaching of Christendom. It accords wonderfully well with the love of God for all mankind that He should have wished those whom He redeemed with the body and blood of His Son to be nourished in some indefinable way by that same flesh and blood and to receive the comfort of his mysterious presence till he returns in glory to be seen by all. I would rather suffer any fate than depart this life with such an awful sin on my conscience as to believe that there is nothing in the mass except bread and wine. Why should I forsake a belief which the Catholic Church has taught for so many centuries? Where do we read "This is not my body but a symbol of my body, this is not my blood but a symbol of my blood"? There is not a single passage which states plainly that the body and blood of our Lord are not present' (1637:39-44, 69-73, 85-105, 128-132).

In considering Erasmus' reaction to the Reformation we should never forget that its success put his life in danger, as was shown by the fate of Louis de Berquin, a young nobleman who was one of King Francis' councillors in Paris, favoured also by Marguerite. Encouraged by a degree of royal support, he had translated *The Handbook of the Christian Soldier* into French along with other books by Erasmus, but without consulting the author. Judging him from his letters to be 'a wise and temperate man', Erasmus wished he had also translated the *Discussion of Free Will*, yet he was anxious enough about what was happening to write to Louis on August 25, 1525. 'I am sure that you meant well, my learned Berquin, when you did what you did, but by translating my books into the vernacular and submitting them to the judgment of the theologians you are increasing the burden of resentment against me, which is already heavy enough. I know there are many good-hearted men amongst the theologians, but the spitefulness of the few often defeats the moderation of the many. I have a natural abhorrence of controversy, and now because of my age and health I desire peace even more, while I make myself ready for that day which cannot now be far off. I see the world embroiled in a deadly conflict; I see the theologians and their opponents carrying their quarrels to the point of utter lunacy. Since I know there is nothing I can do to help, I keep quiet and look after my own affairs, commending Christ's church to him, for he alone knows how to bring good out of the rash purposes of men. Perhaps, my dear Berquin, you will serve your own interests better if you refrain from stirring up an old quarrel again. We are stuck here in Basel. How safe we are, God only knows. I believe the King's sister has already set off for Spain. I have engaged this young man at my own expense to carry my letters and bring back yours in return. Farewell, dear friend' (1599:1-26).

One of the theologians in Paris wrote to warn Erasmus of the hostility aroused. 'Let me tell you what was proposed yesterday about some of your books translated by an admirer of yours when our faculty met in solemn conclave. The men appointed read out from the actual translations anything they had discovered to be unsound. The whole assembly was dumb-founded. They certainly showed no sympathy with your views. I think, dearest brother, that the translator (whom some suspect to be Louis de Berquin) did you no good by his zeal. It is to be feared that you and Lefèvre may share a common fate at the hands of our Masters, for there is no doubt that both of you are the target of frequent and widespread criticism' (1579:200-219). A Dominican alleged that in the *Handbook* Erasmus had not only denied the fires of purgatory but stated that monasticism and piety were not the same thing (1581:853-856).

Erasmus replied at great length to his informant. 'You people are not trying to prevent heresy but to create heretics. I have nothing to do with Berquin, but, if you will let me share with you a little truth, was there any need to include among your criticisms his statement that preachers should invoke the Holy Spirit rather than the Virgin Mary? This, you say, is to insult a commendable practice. Commendable it may be today, but the Fathers knew nothing of this commendable practice. In almost all of the prefaces to his commentaries on the prophets Jerome speaks about invoking the aid of the Holy Spirit, but not of praying to Mary. And supposing the practice is commendable, is it a sin to point out something that is more commendable? It is strange behaviour to endanger the life and reputation of a man like Berquin with petty objections of this sort' (1581:522-536).

But a few months later Berquin was arrested and imprisoned. Thanks to repeated intervention by Marguerite of Angoulême, he survived for three years. Then, when the King was away from Paris, he was quickly condemned and burnt at the stake. Many people deeply influenced by Erasmus, including William Tyndale the great English scholar, were to suffer the same fate.

At the year's end the provost of the cathedral chapter at Constance wrote to Erasmus from Italy. 'Though we have never met, I am not just an admirer of yours but feel a very deep devotion to you who are universally considered one of the wonders of the world. It is because of your remarkable learning that our native Germany, once a boorish and unlettered place, has now burst forth with such splendour and vitality, making the Italians jealous of the great glory which our country has won. For we see among us a constant stream of scholars reaching a remarkable maturity, emerging from your school. When our beloved Germany was in a state of paralysis with nothing on its mind except carousing and drunkenness – which, as you said, was 'the mother of quarrelling, bloodshed, adultery, and almost every crime' (1353:213-214), you brought us to life with your immortal works and now there is hardly an intelligent young man among us who does not think he should devote himself to the refinements of learning. The kindness you show all students emboldens me to send you this letter' (1648:2-20, 31-34).

23

Such a Gift from God

1525: Basel

In 1525 Erasmus still had ten years to live, but the translation of his huge correspondence may not be completed in Toronto before 2020, so it forms a convenient point at which to conclude this investigation of his convictions. Far from being grateful to him for remaining on the papal side, the Catholic Church blamed him for what was happening, rejected his advice for improvement, and placed his writings on the Index of Prohibited Books. Yet once his disapproval of the new movement had become evident, Luther denounced him too and treated him as an enemy. For quite different reasons both Catholics and Protestants have been inclined to belittle him ever since.

The Catholic Church was right in thinking he had been a major influence in bringing about the Reformation. He had certainly prepared the minds of large numbers of Europeans for radical change. The original leaders – Luther, Zwingli, Justus Jonas, Oecolampadius, and many more – were deeply indebted to him. Martin Luther's German New Testament and William Tyndale's English New Testament were translations of Erasmus' Greek New Testament. As the forerunner of the Reformation he can in some respects be compared to John the Baptist, whose profound influence on society is recorded in all four Gospels. Jesus himself said, 'From the days of John the Baptist until now the kingdom of heaven has been taken by storm and eager men are forcing their way into it' (Matt. 11:12). Had Erasmus died at Aachen in 1518, Protestants would gladly have said much the same about him, but he lived on and distanced himself from those who acted upon many of the principles he had advocated.

His astonishing achievements suggest that he was one of the most outstanding European Christians there has ever been. 'If I may speak of myself', he wrote to a distinguished lawyer, the rector of Louvain University, 'I might have rested for some years basking in the kindness of the friends whom the toil I put into my books has won for me in such numbers all the world over, had I not been born into this tragic generation. The less felicity has fallen to my lot here, the greater my confidence that it will be better for me in another world' (1347:335-345). Then he spoke revealingly of his own experiences. 'I was never a slave to sexual gratification and indeed had no time for it under the load of my researches. If I ever had a touch of that trouble I was set free from that tyrant long ago by advancing years. Ambition I always abhorred and now slightly regret this; one should accept in the way of office enough to prevent other men from looking down on one. But in those days I could not imagine that such beasts in human shape existed as I now find. I have no personal ties – such as love of children, parents or kinsfolk – to retain me in this life; I regard with equal affection all who love Christ. I have had a struggle with my spirit to make it adopt a truly Christian feeling towards those who with deliberate spite, like yelping curs, defame a man who deserves none of it and has even served them well. They even plan for my destruction. But I have achieved this. I have no thoughts of revenge. We ought to be equipped with this feeling by the gospel philosophy. As it is, I find it something of a struggle to form in my mind a state of perfect confidence in my own salvation. On this subject I hold frequent debates within myself and sometimes share the problem with learned friends. Nor do I get any satisfaction so far either from Lutherans or anti-Lutherans. And so the wisest course seems to me to be to seek security on this point in every way I can from Christ by prayers and by doing good up to the last day of my life, and then to leave the decision to him, but with the feeling that just as I have the least possible hope from my own merits, so I have great confidence from his immense love towards us and his most generous promises. This is the philosophy by which I now live' (1347:380-415). Having devoted his life to 'the war against wickedness, to which we are summoned beyond a doubt by Christ himself and spurred on by Paul', as well as to 'the teaching of holiness' (335:182-189), he frankly told Pirckheimer, 'I see clearly how weak I am and I do not know to which party to attach myself, except that my conscience gives me some confidence to appear before Jesus my judge' (1268:8-11). Many other senior men – like Pirckheimer and Botzheim – who had a good deal of sympathy for the Reformation but were repelled by the excesses associated with it, also found it beyond them to switch allegiance late in life.

Erasmus originally became famous as a humanist, a champion of the pre-Christian classics rediscovered by Renaissance scholars, yet his first visit to England revealed that he had been a student of Scripture all along. Then when he devoted his life to biblical research he did not abandon the classics, but continued to be a humanist as well, revising and editing the works of many earlier authors. It seems reasonable to suggest that no European has ever equalled his erudition in both secular and sacred literature, in the classics, the New Testament and the church fathers. Widely regarded in his lifetime as 'the greatest scholar in the world' (1594:123), the vast range of his thinking makes him elusive to those who have not had the opportunity to master a proportion of his gigantic output. It was not only intellectuals and professors, students and graduates, schoolboys and teachers who were deeply indebted to him. Multitudes of humbler men and women were delighted to find their experiences and perplexities brilliantly described in enlarged editions of the *Colloquies*. Although he had no sister and never showed any interest in finding a wife for himself, his insight into the problems facing daughters, wives and widows was so remarkable that a substantial volume entitled *Erasmus on Women* was complied in 1996. Notwithstanding his distress at the course of events, his instructive and entertaining books continued to be read all over the continent as well as his Greek New Testament, his Latin New Testament, and his very popular paraphrases, which were later translated into English and attached to the lectern in hundreds of parish churches.

And his correspondence kept consolidating his friendships. 'My dear Erasmus', wrote a law student from Padua in Italy, 'my dear, dear Erasmus. Six of us, all from Flanders, have rented a house together. Your man was here with that thoroughly delightful letter of yours, a pearl to be treasured for all time. At a personal level I cannot measure my gratitude, but I shall try to express it in the only way I know you care about, in my conduct, by making my whole way of life a witness to the power of your books. What evils attend us if we ignore this philosophy, what felicities if we practise it' (1594:1-4, 1650:2-18).

Yet there was a limitation in his character which inclined him to be hostile to other reformers. He was a self-made man who had worked day and night to achieve extraordinary success and fame. Intellectually he became the frontrunner. But when Lefèvre criticised him, he treated him as an opponent in a way which grieved his best friends. In Thomas More's words, 'Never did I admire your eloquence less' (683:36). In Budé's words, 'It is you I am sorry for' (810:333). This prolonged quarrel damaged him, but the same thing happened when he reacted against Edward Lee's disapproval. In Pirckheimer's words, 'You are too big a man to descend into such an arena with men like him' (1095:42). He knew it was damaging him. 'This whole miserable business of Lee has knocked me sideways' (1117:30).

Such antagonisms were not a good preparation for facing Luther, whose protest over indulgences gradually turned into the titanic upheaval of the Reformation. Having stimulated the minds of men to a degree unprecedented for many centuries, Erasmus found himself confronted by someone who was more capable of actually transforming society than he was. Instinctively he held back and avoided studying what Luther wrote. Like everyone else he eventually had to decide whether to applaud or deplore it, but unlike everyone else he was widely considered to be collaborating with him, to be in fact the real author of books and pamphlets published in Luther's name. So his first task was not to evaluate Luther's teaching but to insist that he had nothing whatever to do with it. Yet the similarity between what he had been saying and what Luther had begun to assert was so marked that the theologians in Louvain could not believe him. To them it was obvious that the voice of Luther was the voice of Erasmus. So he was forced to find fault with Luther, if not exactly with what he said, then with the vehement way he said it. Step by step, to avoid intense hostility and even to preserve his life, he was drawn into constant criticism of the reformer and his associates, whether Lutherans or pseudo-Lutherans. As he was still believed to be a ring-leader in the movement his antagonism to it became engrained. So he was eclipsed, robbed of the unique position he had gained, while all eyes turned to Luther.

In 1525 he was 56, equivalent to being 76 today. Brunfels had told him, 'Remember you are old' (1406:262). And Luther, fourteen years his junior, had said, 'I wish the papists might cease to attack you so fiercely and might allow you in your old age peacefully to fall asleep in the Lord' (1443:55-57).

If, instead of changing his tune, Erasmus had contrived to encourage the reformers by his friendship, advice and criticism, sharing with them the risk of being burnt alive, he would never have passed into the unhappiness which marred his later years. Instead of being Oecolampadius' opponent, he could have been his colleague in the successful struggle to capture Basel for the reformed faith. But he failed to realize that times had changed and younger men with God-given abilities and vision had taken over the leadership which used to be his. To this day Protestants have tended to remember how he lost his way in the storm of events when he was elderly and ill, forgetting the immense achievements of his prime.

Like Luther, Erasmus was not devoid of shortcomings, but his greatness was so exceptional that he remains an inspiring model of Christian discipleship. Quite apart from his disciplined behaviour, the huge number of books he wrote or edited, and his unique service in establishing, translating, and explaining the text of the New Testament, we ought to remember how staunchly he maintained that morality is part of theology, that faith includes obedience, and that the redeeming death of Christ must never be separated from the teaching of Christ, for together they reveal one gospel, one comprehensive Christian philosophy by which we should live. Five hundred years on, we are the heirs of what he achieved, and we need to make fuller use of such a gift from God as that academic orphan from Rotterdam.

Index of Selected Subjects

Index of People and Places

Index of Erasmus' writings mentioned

Flavius
JOSEPHUS
A UNIQUE WITNESS
Independent Evidence confirming the New Testament Story
This is a helpful introduction to an important first century historian. It concentrates on how his writings relate to the New Testament, frequently confirming its history and illuminating its context.
Oliver Barclay, Leicester
David Bentley-Taylor

Josephus, A Unique Witness

Independent Evidence confirming the New Testament Story

David Bentley-Taylor

Is there any extra-biblical data about the times in which Jesus lived?

Thanks to Josephus, the religious, social and political environment familiar to Jesus and the apostles springs to life in his pages. Here is a readable selection from his extensive writings, confirming the New Testament documents.

'Josephus was a first century Jew living in Jerusalem during most of the events recorded in the Acts of the Apostles... Josephus was not a Christian, but he knew about John the Baptist and Jesus... He was a man of action and a talented historian, describing in detail the terrible struggle between the Romans and the Jews in which he himself played so significant a role.'

'*This is a helpful introduction to an important first century historian. It concentrates on how his writings relate to the New Testament, frequently confirming its history and illuminating its context.*'

Dr Oliver Barclay

'David Bentley-Taylor has done an excellent job in reviewing the works of Josephus and particularly bringing to out attention the points at which Josephus's account touches on the background to the NT an incidents we find there.'

Evangelicals Now

ISBN 1 85792 499 1

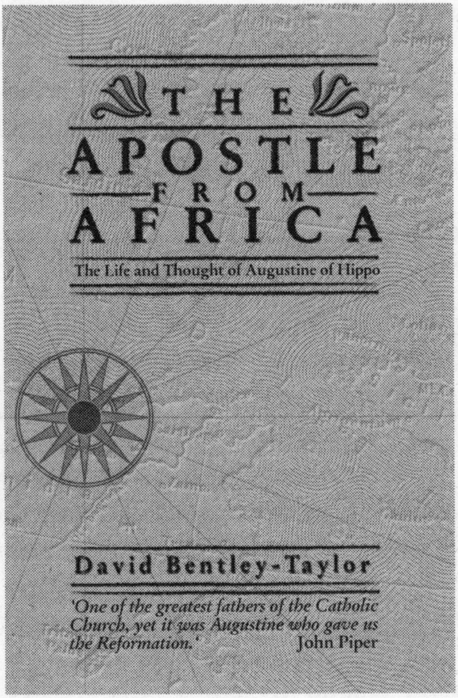
THE
APOSTLE
FROM
AFRICA
The Life and Thought of Augustine of Hippo
David Bentley-Taylor
'One of the greatest fathers of the Catholic Church, yet it was Augustine who gave us the Reformation.' John Piper

The Apostle from Africa

The Life and Thought of Augustine of Hippo

David Bentley Taylor

'One of greatest fathers of the Catholic Church, yet it was Augustine who gave us the Reformation.' John Piper

Born 700 years after Plato and dying 400 years after Jesus' crucifixion, Augustine was an outstanding Christian thinker. Around the Mediterranean leading men hung on his words. At times his errors were deplorable, even horrifying, yet Augustine grew up to be the man who has influenced the church more than any other extra-Biblical writer.

Augustine is cherished as a father of the Roman Catholic Church but also influenced the Reformation - not only because Luther was an Augustinian monk, or that Calvin quoted Augustine more than any other theologian, but because the Reformation witnessed the triumph of Augustine's doctrine of grace.

He was such a brilliant teacher that by the time he was thirty he had been a professor at three universities. His knowledge of history and literature, personal experience of human distress and his strong convictions gave him the Roman Empire as his congregation.

We learn how he was overwhelmed by sexual immorality as a teenager yet once he became a Christian he attained an astonishing mastery of the scriptures – forcing him to spend the next forty years as a preacher and magistrate by day, an author and controversialist by night. His first biographer, a lifelong colleague, dared to say *"Augustine lives forever"*, and he was not wrong.

"Augustine entered both the Church and the world as a revolutionary force, and not merely created an epoch in the history of the Church, but... determined the course of its history in the West up to the present day. The whole development of Western life, in all its phases, was powerfully affected by his teaching."

B.B. Warfield

Includes an introduction to Augustine by John Piper

ISBN 1 85792 4711

Christian Focus Publications publishes books for all ages

Our mission statement -

STAYING FAITHFUL
In dependence upon God we seek to help make his infallible word, the Bible, relevant. Our aim is to ensure that the Lord Jesus Christ is presented as the only hope to obtain forgiveness of sin, live a useful life and look forward to heaven with him.

REACHING OUT
Christ's last command requires us to reach out to our world with his gospel. We seek to help fulfill that by publishing books that point people towards Jesus and for them to develop a Christ-like maturity. We aim to equip all levels of readers for life, work ministry and mission.

Books in our adult range are published in three imprints.

Christian Heritage contains classic writings from the past.
Mentor focuses on books written at a level suitable for Bible College and seminary students, pastors, and other serious readers; the imprint includes commentaries, doctrinal studies, examination of current issues, and church history.
Christian Focus contains popular works including biographies, commentaries, basic doctrine, and Christian living. Our children's books are also published in this imprint.

For a free catalogue of all our titles, please write to

Christian Focus Publications, Ltd
Geanies House, Fearn,
Ross-shire, IV20 1TW, Scotland, United Kingdom

For details of our titles visit us on our website
www.christianfocus.com